Future HUSBAND, Present PRAYERS

Future HUSBAND, *Present* PRAYERS

HOW PRAYING WHILE YOU WAIT
TRANSFORMS YOUR SINGLENESS
AND PREPARES YOU FOR MARRIAGE

CHRISTIAN BEVERE

W Publishing Group
An Imprint of Thomas Nelson

Future Husband, Present Prayers

Published in Nashville, Tennessee, by W Publishing, an imprint of Thomas Nelson. W Publishing and Thomas Nelson are registered trademarks of HarperCollins Christian Publishing, Inc.

Thomas Nelson titles may be purchased in bulk for educational, business, fundraising, or sales promotional use. For information, please email SpecialMarkets@ThomasNelson.com.

ISBN 978-1-4003-5175-6 (audiobook)
ISBN 978-1-4003-5174-9 (eBook)
ISBN 978-1-4003-5173-2 (TP)

HarperCollins Publishers, Macken House, 39/40 Mayor Street Upper, Dublin 1, D01 C9W8, Ireland (https://www.harpercollins.com)

Library of Congress Control Number: 2025943105

Printed in the United States of America
26 27 28 29 30 LBC 7 6 5 4 3

To my husband, Arden:

When you were my future husband, I prayed that God would bring me a person to love and partner with through this adventure called life. Now as my husband, father to our children, and faithful leader, I've seen those prayers answered in even greater ways than I could have imagined.

Thank you for being my sharpener, my joy-increaser, my best friend, my muse, and my biggest supporter in writing this book. As we continue to discover God's goodness and watch the power of prayer unfold over our lives in the years to come, I'm thankful that it's you whose side I'll be next to.

You're so out of my league that God had to have heard my prayers! I love you yesterday, today, and tomorrow.

CONTENTS

PART 3: WHAT TO PRAY

FOREWORD

I distinctly remember the first time I saw Christian. I met her on her first date with our son Arden when our family was on a brief vacation in Florida. She was beautiful, but I immediately knew there was something different, something more to her. I not only saw it in her, I saw it reflected in my son. What began as an early afternoon coffee date blossomed into a whole-day event. Even though she came from an all-girl family, she had no problem holding her own in games along with Arden's brothers. As a mother to four sons, I can attest that competitive games and athletics are a given in our family. Arden and Christian faced a challenge, though: Our family lived in Colorado, and Christian lived in Alabama.

Long-distance relationships are either made in or broken by the separation. From the beginning, Christian let Arden know she wasn't interested in moving forward with him if he was a player. She had no way of knowing that Arden was ready to marry. He had recently shared this with us even before meeting Christian. He knew marriage was a deep commitment and a catalyst for growth. For some time, he had been preparing himself to build a life with someone.

I remember there were long hours with Arden in his room on FaceTime with Christian. Together they read the Bible and books that would deepen their relationship with their Lord and with one another.

They dreamed together. It wasn't long before they were engaged and, shortly after that, married.

On their wedding day Christian gifted Arden the Bible she had read, journaled in, and prayed through when the idea of marriage was but a dream. For years and through tears she had sown seeds of faith, hope, and love into their future, long before their paths crossed. I can't imagine a treasure more precious.

I've had the privilege of watching Christian love my son. She is an extraordinary mother first to a son and now to their daughter. She loves John and me as a daughter would. She could be happy moving forward and enjoying her very full life, but she has faithfully carried in her heart the women who find themselves in a season of wondering and waiting. What began as a podcast grew into a community and now the book you hold. More than a how-to, this book is a guide of "Who-to." Through the living Word of God, we discover our heavenly Father is our refuge. Jesus is the ultimate Bridegroom, the One we bring our longings and fears to, knowing He understands. And the Holy Spirit is the One who we can trust to counsel us. The prayers and principles woven into each page of this book have blessed our lives and built Arden and Christian's family.

Be encouraged: For each of us who have set our hearts on Jesus, there is indeed the hope of an eternal future Husband, and we have the honor of growing into the likeness of His Bride.

—LISA BEVERE

New York Times Bestselling Author

PART 1

WHY TO *Pray*

Introduction

WHY SHOULD YOU PRAY FOR YOUR FUTURE HUSBAND?

Picture this: You've just graduated from college and thought you'd have a ring on your finger and a job offer in your inbox. But without either, you're watching as your friends are landing their dream jobs and picking out rings with their soon-to-be fiancés. You, on the other hand, accept a job in your hometown and begin feeling like the single and singled-out friend.

Maybe you don't have to try very hard to picture that scenario because it feels all too familiar. That's how I felt in the fall of 2013. I was watching friends try on wedding dresses and accept contracts for their dream careers—while I was packing up my college apartment and accepting the reality that I was moving back to my hometown.

No ring on my finger. No job offers in my inbox. Just me, my degree, and a very full car heading back to sweet home Alabama.

And while I was genuinely happy for my friends (really! I even brought cupcakes to the bridal showers), I couldn't shake the ache of feeling like the single, slightly-left-behind friend.

On my drive home, I thought about the postgrad life I had always pictured—something a little more cinematic. I'd meet my husband in college, get engaged by senior year, then move to an exciting city—maybe fall in love in New York or have my own Hollywood meet-cute. You know, the kind of story that you pay to go see.

My daydreaming slowed as the exits became more recognizable—Cracker Barrel on the right, beach twenty miles ahead—and reality hit me harder than the slap of humidity on a Southern summer day. I had spent four years at college only to come back to work my old job in my hometown. And despite what every Hallmark movie promised, there was no flannel-wearing ex waiting for me with a sweet tea and a second chance at love.

I couldn't help but feel the tension of where I was in contrast to where I'd pictured I would be. I started wondering if the dreams I'd held on to for so long were still possible . . . or if they were just wishful thinking dressed up as a plan.

So there I was, living back at home and getting ready for my not-so-first first day at my former job. Now don't get me wrong, I had loved that role. It was a successful online boutique where I excelled in business management and creative design—a dream for my inner fashionista! But I thought that role was for *high school* me, not *postgrad* me. Postgrad Christian was supposed to have a journalism degree and an MRS degree; she was supposed to be starting a new job at a major broadcast company in a big city while planning a Pinterest-worthy wedding in Italy. Isn't it funny how fast hopeful expectations can turn into quiet doubts when life doesn't follow the timeline we imagined? I thought I'd be crossing off milestones. Instead, I was circling back. And yet—somehow—that's exactly where God started to do something new.

On my first day back at work, my boss gave me an odd assignment: meet the girl who'd been filling my old position. Before I officially stepped back in—and she stepped out to go back to school for cosmetology—our boss arranged a brunch meetup for the two of us. Why? I wondered. Was this some kind of secret second interview? Or was she having second thoughts about leaving and wanted to size me up? I was skeptical of the whole setup (and clearly had a few trust issues to work through). But Mary Payne—MP as I'd come to call her—and I hit it off from the start and quickly became close friends. Maybe my boutique boss could double as a successful "friend-finder" or matchmaker.

This wasn't a sneaky setup; it was a God setup! As MP and I chatted over coffee and pancakes, I found that I wasn't the only one whose post-grad plans didn't perfectly fit their expectations and was left wondering how to navigate the career and dating scenes. We decided not only were we going to enjoy and make the most of this season, but we were going to have preemptive joy for the next one too.

It can be easy to believe we can't have joy in singleness unless we downplay or abandon our desire for marriage, or that joy about marriage only begins when we have a ring on our finger. But what if we could bridge that gap? What if we could enjoy our time of singleness *and* enjoy what we believe is to come?

MP and I spent our work trips dreaming of what the future could hold, admittedly drinking too many Starbucks lattes and blaring "I Could Use a Love Song" by Maren Morris (because boy, could we!). It was greatly beneficial to have someone to journey with in that season. Notice I say to *journey* with—not to complain with or to distract each other (though they are the more tempting first approaches).

We walked through the tension of this season side by side—sharing our frustrations but never letting them define us. In the middle of the waiting and the questioning, we kept reminding each other of what we were truly believing for: purpose-filled careers and deeply rooted relationships. Through prayer, honest conversations, and the kind of friendship that holds you up when your faith feels shaky, we helped each other stay grounded.

Hope wasn't always loud, but it was steady—and together, we kept our eyes on the bigger story God was writing. Even when I was doubting that God could bring me a radical love story, I never doubted it for my friend. And if she ever started to doubt it, I'd shut it down faster than a bad date: "Girl, you're a catch. You don't do *mehs*, *maybes*, or 'he's got potential.' Your worthwhile love story is in the making!"

We became each other's hope dealers. When one of us couldn't see it, the other spoke it aloud. And can I tell you something? That kind of belief—unapologetic, fiercely loyal, and slightly dramatic—blessed me more than I knew.

We had a Proverbs 27:17 type of friendship—sharpening each other to hold fast to our beliefs and share our convictions. So you can imagine how I felt when MP got into a cosmetology program—four hours away.

I was thrilled for my friend and glad the Lord was opening the next door for her, but we were sad that we wouldn't get to do life near each other anymore. I wondered: Could we keep holding each other accountable? What would we do when we were alone and the temptation to lose hope or settle crept in?

The night before she moved, we sat in her room—packing her boxes and planning how to keep the seeds we had planted growing. I was already losing proximity to my friend; I didn't want to lose this hope we'd built too. FaceTime catch-ups and weekend visits would be nice, but I found myself wishing we had something more deliberate. Something that would keep us both tethered in our friendship and in our new hope—but *what*?

Then it hit us.

And the LORD answered me: "Write the vision; make it plain on tablets, so he may run who reads it. For still the vision awaits its appointed time; it hastens to the end—it will not lie. If it seems slow, wait for it; it will surely come; it will not delay." (Hab. 2:2–3)

We decided that we would keep the vision for our marriages alive by writing a letter to each other's future husband. This way, we not only had our own beliefs of the character and qualities our future partner would hold, but we got to pair them with each other's declarations as well.

We whipped out pen and paper and started jotting down sentiments of gratitude and proclamations of faith, thanking God for our friend's future spouse and addressing the letter to the other's groom on their wedding day. It was purposeful, prophetic, and profound.

As MP and I started writing, it marked an innovation in our vision for the future, one that no longer lived alone in our heads but was now imprinted with words. Though I had no clue who my future husband would be, and sometimes still doubted my dream guy would find me in lower Alabama, I now had a letter from a friend who didn't have the answers but had joined in faith that this man was coming. Before,

I could talk myself out of my own hopes for my husband by chalking them up to fickle fairy-tale thoughts of love, but now, seeing a letter of belief addressed in pen to the man I would marry, my desires didn't feel like fiction; they felt more like faith.

It was riveting. We wanted more.

What if this solo letter wasn't the only thing I'd one day give my husband? Could I keep transforming my fickle thoughts into tangible actions of faith? Maybe, just maybe, we could make this a continuous action. We decided to create what I like to call the "Husband Bible." First, I scanned Amazon for a dudish Bible. *Hmm . . . What would my future husband like?* I asked myself. (It's a little daunting to pick a gift for someone you've never met!) When a classic brown leather Bible popped up, I added it to my cart, and the Husband's Bible journey began.

MP and I prayed over and wrote in these Bibles that we planned to give to our future husbands. They became a staple in our journey and a tool for restored hope.

After going on my own hunt, I created a resource, the Dear Future Husband Prayer Journal, that you can use as your own.

ME, MYSELF, AND MY HUSBAND'S BIBLE

With my friend now four hours away, the lonely weekend nights and Instagram doomscrolls stirred the old temptation to rush through my single season. But on the rare occasion I'd get asked out, I'd go back to my dedicated Bible and start praying for my future husband, and it'd make it much harder to convince myself that it was okay to start down the wrong path. If I was praying for a man of strong conviction and shared faith, it'd be an obvious "Girl, what are you doing?" moment if I said "yes" to dating someone I knew, or learned, wasn't portraying those characteristics. My standards and convictions became stronger and stronger.

I began *contending* for my desire for a husband rather than merely *hoping* for it.

I started bringing God into the conversation around my relationships—this time *before* I caught feelings. Why do we like to wait until we're in our feelings to begin asking for wisdom? Praying things like, "God, if this isn't it, give me a sign" but conveniently ignoring all the red flags He already sent. Inviting God in *early* can save you a lot of confusion later—and bring much more peace along the way. And honestly, it was so refreshing. There was more clarity, less chaos, and way fewer "what was I thinking?" moments.

I discovered a new layer of trust and joy in my relationship with God. A vulnerability and release. Rather than continuing to think I had to find the perfect relationship to make God happy, I realized I needed to bring my imperfections to Him and let Him find the right relationship for me. I'd pray for my future husband continually and laugh through the pain of my bad dating track record, telling God, "Look, I've made a mess of my emotions and love life, so I'm going to need You to walk me through this like I'm blind!"

That's exactly what God does, isn't it? Directs our steps best when we follow Him with blind obedience. You and I cannot fully anticipate what lies ahead, but with each step we take, we inch closer to the good things He has waiting around the corner.

In their hearts humans plan their course,
but the Lord establishes their steps. (Prov. 16:9 NIV)

Now, I'm not going to lie to you. The Bible doesn't promise us marriage. But it *does* promise that God's presence is with us and that He hears our prayers. As 1 Peter 3:12 reminds us, "The eyes of the Lord are on the righteous, and his ears are open to their prayer."

The truth is, we're not always privy to the when, where, and who.

But in this book I want to encourage you to be actively praying through the *why*, *how*, and *what* of believing for your future husband. I want to encourage you: Whether you meet your dream guy tomorrow or God leads you to fulfill other dreams first, this journey won't be wasted. Part of praying is seeking—drawing near and finding ourselves fulfilled in Him. The relationship you cultivate with the Lord in learning to depend on and trust in Him is worth it. Wherever you find yourself today, I am really glad you picked up this book—no matter what your *why* was!

A combination of delay and doubt can lead our fears to whisper, *If it hasn't happened yet, will it ever?* So how can we handle our doubts in a hope-filled way? Some of you may be so weary and worn down from yet another Hinge fail or blind-date setup that you're struggling to believe God really does have a husband in store for you. Or you might wonder whether this journey of learning *why*, *how*, and *what* to pray for your future husband will end up being even more wasted time if marriage isn't in store for you. Maybe you haven't started dating yet (in which case, hats off to you for wanting to do things with wisdom from the start!). Or maybe a loved one just shoved this book in your hands. No matter what brought you here, I hope this journey brings you closer to the Lord and empowers you to turn your season of singleness—which can feel like a time of passive waiting—into active transformation through surrendering your future marriage and current relationship status to the Lord.

And while I can't promise you'll have a husband by page 100 (if only it worked like that!), I *can* promise that this book will help guide your prayers and strengthen your connection with the One who holds your future. We'll dive into how to pray for your future husband, how to date with wisdom, and, most importantly, how to keep your heart anchored in faith every step of the way.

I'm proud of you for showing up for this journey—and excited to see what God does with your "yes." Let's get started!

CHAPTER 1

BECAUSE BREAKTHROUGH AWAITS

As teenage girls stepping into young womanhood—full of hormones, baseless confidence, and a wild craving for independence—we thought we knew everything, didn't we?

With a driver's license in one hand and a flip phone in the other, we began the task of trying to form who we were and what we were about. Which, let's be real, was less about our character and motives and more about finding our style, friend groups, and, of course, our crushes.

Back when our most pressing problems were predicaments such as, "Should I wear my gaucho pants or my miniskirt with neon leggings to get Jake to make me his bae?"

Cringe.

And while we were busy rolling our eyes and insisting, "You just don't understand, Mom," somehow, she did . . . a little too well. My mom could sniff out a shady friend or a no-good boyfriend right away.

I'm glad we didn't make bets on who would stick around because I'd have owed her a pretty penny. Looking back with a little more wisdom (and plenty of awkward stories and revelations), I realize I should have heeded her advice.

Sometimes mama really *does* know best!

The most quoted chapter in the Bible on how to be a godly woman and godly wife is Proverbs 31, and for good reason. And while there is beneficial wisdom to gain from this passage for how to act and carry ourselves as women, I believe there's deeper insight available.

> Listen, my son! Listen, son of my womb! Listen, my son, the answer to my prayers... A wife of noble character who can find? She is worth far more than rubies. Her husband has full confidence in her and lacks nothing of value. She brings him good, not harm, all the days of her life. . . . She is clothed with strength and dignity; she can laugh at the days to come. She speaks with wisdom, and faithful instruction is on her tongue. She watches over the affairs of her household and does not eat the bread of idleness. Her children arise and call her blessed; her husband also, and he praises her: "Many women do noble things, but you surpass them all." Charm is deceptive, and beauty is fleeting; but a woman who fears the LORD is to be praised.
>
> —PROVERBS 31:2, 10–12, 25–30 NIV

This passage contains more than quotable verses for an Instagram story and goes deeper than a poetic tribute to an ideal woman—it is a mother's instruction to her son in his search and selection of his bride. It is insight from an older woman of wisdom for the younger women after her. If we study it intentionally, it is a wealth of knowledge and a model for feminine righteousness.

The very first piece of wisdom we receive from this chapter isn't instruction for how we should act, look, or speak as women; it's that we should pray! Before she gives him a single utterance of what to look for in a spouse directly, she indirectly shows that a woman of godly love is one who prays. She asked God for this son of her womb, and God answered her prayer. She believed for her child, this future king, and asked God for the fulfillment of her desire and the blessing of his formation.

That same kind of raw, honest prayer can apply to our desire for marriage too—different request, same faithful God.

LAUGHING THROUGH THE LONGING

In Genesis, Sarah set an example of praying for her heart's desire that reminds us you're never too old (or too humble) to be used by God. When three angels came to her and her husband, Abraham, to share that she would be a mother to nations, she laughed. Seriously, she LOL'd right there in front of the divine messengers. When I read this, I envision *The Princess Diaries* scene where Mia responds to her royal grandmother's news of her genealogy by saying, "Me? A princess? Shut up!"[1] But Sarah wasn't a teenage girl struck by shock like Mia; she was a ninety-year-old woman of the desert. Her days had been tiresome and her decades of waiting for a child had been prolonged. So much time had passed that she truly couldn't believe the words she was hearing and counted herself out from this blessing and promise.

But God's math is different from ours, because what would be humanly impossible or implausible to us is never an issue for Him. A woman's typical childbearing years end in her forties. Yet, He saw Sarah, who was way past that mark, and said, "Now's the time, and she is the one!"

That's how God works oftentimes, isn't it? Right when we think there's surely no way our dreams will come true, He shifts the tide. Coming to the end of our own strength and learning to rely on God is an intentional aspect of faith. Once we let go of control, we begin to move fully in faith.

I picture Sarah past the window of frustration and anger. She'd cried all the tears she had left. Now, she was laughing—signaling her faith had dried up with her tears.

Are there any dreams or desires that feel hard-fought or forgotten? Is there a prayer you've been waiting to see answered that you've gotten angry with God about, or even cried about? He knows. And He will *lovingly* call it out for your good. The angels called out Sarah's response, asking Abraham why she laughed at receiving this good news.

Like I admittedly might have done, she said, "Who, me? Nope, no laughing over here!"

But the angels said, "Girl, yes. Stop lying" (Gen. 18:15, my paraphrase).

I believe something awoke again in Sarah whenever she was challenged. Presented with a new hope, she had the realization that nothing is over unless God says so. He *can* and *is willing to* work all things out for good for those who believe in Him (Rom. 8:28).

Maybe you feel like tapping out now, but I encourage you to lean in—even with all the emotions your waiting has brought. For Sarah, her first response of laughing eventually turned into true joy. Genesis 21 recounts, "Sarah said, 'God has brought me laughter, and everyone who hears about this will laugh with me.' And she added, 'Who would have said to Abraham that Sarah would nurse children? Yet I have borne him a son in his old age'" (vv. 6–7 NIV).

Not only did she become pregnant, but she delivered Isaac—the first son in the lineage that led to Jesus. I love how Hebrews 11 says it: "By faith Sarah herself received power to conceive, even when she was past the age, since she considered him faithful who had promised" (v. 11). Take special notice of that last line: She considered *Him* faithful! While doubt and practicality had convinced her she was too old to conceive, ultimately her spirit rested in the faith that God is faithful to fulfill His promises.

If, like Sarah, your heart feels weary to the point of laughing at what you once prayed for, please do not lose hope. Her story shows that our waiting is never in vain because nothing is over until God says so. Even if you have counted yourself out, God has not tapped out.

And Sarah's story is not the only example of God's faithfulness in Scripture.

Marked as infertile, Hannah contended for a child. She was a godly woman and deeply loved by her husband, yet they had been unable to become pregnant. This wrecked her to a level not even her husband could understand or empathize with. As men like to do, he tried to fix the problem and encouraged her by saying things like, "My lovely wife, eat and be happy! You are loved and you have me!" (1 Sam. 1:8, my paraphrase). But while sweet words and soul food can lift our spirits for a moment, no savory dish can substitute for those deep longings of the heart.

To make things even worse, Hannah's husband's *other* wife (thank goodness that tradition didn't make it to the twenty-first century!) could have children—and she made sure Hannah never forgot it. First Samuel 1:6 tells us this "sister-wife" seemed to have one mission in life: to poke, prod, and pester Hannah to the point of depleting her faith. I can just imagine her taunts: "You've never been pregnant and never will get pregnant. Yet look at all my children I have borne for our husband!" I can envision Hannah covering her ears and turning her face while her heart broke a little more with each taunt. Maybe she even began to ask herself, *Is she right?*

Yet I'm stirred by Hannah's response through all the waiting, the taunting, and others' inability to understand what she was going through. Because while I would have let those remarks knock me down and probably tried to blame it all on my husband in a failed attempt at feeling less broken, she didn't. Remarkably, she let the delays and doubts *shape* her faith rather than *strip* it.

One day, when her pain was paramount, she ran to the temple to seek refuge in God. The priest Eli found her praying so fervently he believed her to be drunk. "Put your wine away," he called out (1 Sam. 1:14). Can you imagine taking your pain through prayer to God and your pastor walks in accusing you of day drinking? The audacity, sir! Hannah enlightened him that she hadn't been pouring a drink but was pouring out her heart to the Lord: "I have been praying here out of my great anguish and grief" (v. 16 NIV).

You may relate to her downcast heart all too well. Perhaps doubt has grown as you've watched what feels like all the good options for a spouse be claimed, or have been unintentionally taunted by well-meaning friends and family asking about your love life or relationship status. Or maybe this is a raw gut check, where you realize you have been crying in disappointment rather than crying out in faith. My friend, let yourself feel all the emotions that come with dating and waiting, but don't let them steal your faith.

See, Hannah admitted to her loved ones and to God that she had unfulfilled desires and they were taking a toll on her heart. That's okay! And it's okay for you to pray for the desire of a husband and be honest with God about where you're at. Why do we feel we have to either be completely content on our own in singleness or a heartbroken cat lady wallowing in self-pity? Friend, the Lord can handle our bold feelings, and He is not offended when we lament to Him. Moreover, He welcomes it (Ps. 130:1)! Because what happens if we don't? If we sweep things under the rug or run on fumes for too long, that's when our faith tank can run out of gas. So take a page from Hannah's book, because the waiting isn't always easy, but ease isn't what leads to answers!

Hannah's story also shows that our hope does not depend on being understood or quickly getting answers—our hope rests solely on Christ. After years of believing for something that still hadn't happened, and seemed likely it never could, Hannah cried out even more fervently. She took her requests to God for a child and pleaded, "LORD Almighty, if you will only look on your servant's misery and remember me, and not forget your servant but give her a son, then I will give him to the LORD for all the days of his life" (1 Sam. 1:11 NIV).

I love that the Word says the Lord *remembered* Hannah (v. 19). He remembered the times she met Him in her longing in the secret place, how she lamented in her grief while standing in faith. He remembered the sound of a woman worshiping her God and answered her song with gladness. Her womb, which was once closed, was now carrying the precious by-product of faith—a son. This steadfast woman cemented this beautifully in the name she bestowed on her son: Samuel, which means, "I have asked for him from the LORD" (v. 20).

YOU HAVE NOT BECAUSE YOU ASK NOT

If you desire marriage, don't be afraid to ask it of God. If we are encouraged to pray for our children, nations, and even strangers, you best believe we are going to pray for our husbands too!

Sometimes we worry that asking God for something—especially a partner—makes us selfish or ungrateful. But Hannah's story shows us God does not dismiss the daughter who comes to him asking, "Father, please!" In fact, Scripture says God receives the prayers of the ones who remain in righteousness and believe in what they ask (Matt. 21:22; Prov. 15:29).

Like the mothers in the Bible who poured out their hopes and prayers with passion and trust, you, too, can bring your longing to God wholeheartedly.

Maybe you're like I was at first—nervous to ask God to bring you a husband. I wondered, *Do I deserve a godly guy? Would asking such a thing be distasteful or rebellious?* But then I realized: God already knows what's in my heart. So why be shy about sharing it with Him? Surely bringing Him into that desire would be more pleasing, and powerful, than dating in my own effort or hiding that desire away.

Think of your desire for a spouse like planting a flower seed. There's a time for it to be planted and hidden, but eventually, it needs to push toward the sunlight to bloom. Our desire for a spouse is the same—it can't stay hidden forever if it's going to grow. Sometimes it's okay to be in a season of healing or waiting quietly, but when your heart is ready, that seed needs to come into the light. I had kept this desire hidden in my heart, stuck in the dirt, while expecting it to bloom. No wonder my dating had been messy! I needed God's partnership—His watering of wisdom and light of insight. Bringing our prayers to God is like exposing seeds to sunlight and water. When we plant in faith, He brings it to fruition!

Some might ask, "But isn't the heart deceitful above all else? Wouldn't my desires be selfish?" That is a real possibility, and a good awareness to have. How do we proceed in prayer for our heart's desire without letting desire itself taint our ask? Let's glean from James 4: "What causes fights and quarrels among you? Don't they come from your desires that battle within you? You desire but do not have, so you kill. You covet but you cannot get what you want, so you quarrel and fight. You do not have because you do not ask God. When you ask, you do not receive, because you ask with wrong motives, that you may spend what you get on your pleasures" (vv. 1–3 NIV).

> BRINGING OUR PRAYERS TO GOD IS LIKE EXPOSING SEEDS TO SUNLIGHT AND WATER. WHEN WE PLANT IN FAITH, HE BRINGS IT TO FRUITION!

I don't think these verses encourage us to pretend we do not hold desires; rather, James was telling us to submit them to God's will. We cry out for a godly marriage in God's will because we fear God.

The more I buried my hope for a husband, the more I felt restless or hopeless and would act and date in ways contrary to what I wanted. I'd become jealous of my friends' relationships and quicker to go on a date I didn't have peace about, or I would feel lonesome in my singleness. What good was my desire doing in my own hands and working through my own wisdom?

When we keep our desire to ourselves and only want it for ourselves, then it is a flesh desire, but when we present it to God and ask for it in His will, it can become fruitful. James continues with this reminder, and I love the way The Message paraphrases it:

> You're cheating on God. If all you want is your own way, flirting with the world every chance you get, you end up enemies of God and his way. And do you suppose God doesn't care? The proverb has it that "he's a fiercely jealous lover." And what he gives in love is far better than anything else you'll find. It's common knowledge that "God goes against the willful proud; God gives grace to the willing humble."
>
> So let God work his will in you. Yell a loud *no* to the Devil and watch him make himself scarce. Say a quiet *yes* to God and he'll be there in no time. Quit dabbling in sin. Purify your inner life. Quit playing the field. Hit bottom, and cry your eyes out. The fun and games are over. Get serious, really serious. Get down on your knees before the Master; it's the only way you'll get on your feet. (4:4–10)

This first part of the book focuses on why to pray for your future husband, so this is your time to get serious about your *why*. Are you seeking this desire so you can get out of singleness or because you believe in kingdom marriage? Are you asking for a husband because you think having someone will bring you happiness or because you believe there is purpose in partnership? If you're like I was, you could be somewhere in the middle. Let your desire be purified through prayer. Desires can be faltered and self-seeking when kept in passion but can be purified and powerful through prayer.

I believe praying for your future husband benefits you two as a couple, but it greatly benefits you as an individual as well. Confident, ceaseless prayers deepen our dependency and dispel our doubts. Even before we see any proof of what we're asking for, the Bible says these petitions we send forth to God are working our faith greater than our eyes seeing their fulfillment. Prayer isn't just a last resort; it's a powerful resource!

Ask boldly, believingly, without a second thought. People who "worry their prayers" are like wind-whipped waves. Don't think you're going to get anything from the Master that way, adrift at sea, keeping all your options open. (James 1:6–8 MSG)

When I changed my *why*, it changed me.

By contending for the marriage I longed for regularly and writing down my "Dear Future Husband" prayers and letters, faith sprung forth within me. I realized I'd made relationships comfort blankets rather than centering them on covenant purpose. It transformed how I approached my desires and the longing itself. And, honestly, it's still changing me. Because with every new season and challenge we come up against in our marriage, I go back to that reminder: My marriage isn't just for me; my marriage is a ministry.

> CONFIDENT, CEASELESS PRAYERS DEEPEN OUR DEPENDENCY AND DISPEL OUR DOUBTS.

Before, I'd pray for a husband while holding my breath until I turned blue—but this awareness changed my perspective. I was ready to hit my knees consistently and pray for God to aid him and sharpen us both until the right time for us to be together arose, should it be His will. I was filled with joy at this change in the tide, but the next step I needed to confront was, *What did this look like? How does one wait* well*?*

I'm sure that's the sole reason someone bought this book—to discover how to believe in faith but contend in contentedness. Or maybe you don't want to wait well; you'd rather not wait at all! Friend, I get it. And while I cannot promise a three-step formula or a flawless path—as much as I wish I could—we can uncover the applicable, unfailing wisdom from the Word that directs us even in the waiting. Let's walk together into the heart of that tension—between desire and surrender, hope and patience—and uncover how you can actually and authentically wait *well.*

CHAPTER 2

BECAUSE WAITING WELL DOESN'T JUST HAPPEN

I'm convinced that no experience shapes how you wait like going to the DMV.

The Department of Motor Vehicles' abbreviation could more accurately stand for *Deliberately Moving Very slowly* or *Dread Meets Visitors*. Welcome! Please take a number and a chill pill.

Let me jump ahead a bit to a story from my marriage that may bring you comfort in your single or dating season. A few years into our marriage, around 2021, Arden and I sensed the peace that God was releasing us from Colorado and calling us to the South. And let me tell you, this Alabama-born-and-raised girl was thrilled! The day we moved to Tennessee is forever ingrained in my mind. Waking up to the lush green trees and singing birds flooded me with joy. Now I know there will be some mountain gals reading this, and Colorado is beautiful, but

I'm a Southern girl who loves her open fields and Southern slowness. Tennessee already felt like home!

But apparently, according to the state, it's not quite home until you fill out the necessary paperwork and government documents to legally establish residency—most of which we did right away, except for my driver's license.

It wasn't until three years after we moved I realized I finally needed to visit the dreaded DMV. I went mentally prepared to sit in an uncomfortable plastic chair for an hour or two until I could get my new picture taken and receive my license to officially be a Tennessean. But I was not prepared for what followed . . .

After waiting in line to see the clerk, I was turned away and told I needed to come back with different paperwork. So I did. But then I was turned away again . . . and again . . . and again. Eight times I went back and forth! I began this DMV journey in my third trimester, and by my eighth trip, I had a newborn as my copilot.

Every time, there was another reason I had to wait in line only to be turned away. I'd tried everything, even switching between going with an appointment and going as a walk-in. Whatever I did, nothing worked.

I called my husband crying driving home from that seventh failed attempt. I was so frustrated at repeat ventures with no resolve, having no clarity on what to do differently. And it was easy to cry. It was easy to get ticked at the system or at the workers who gave me mixed information. But none of those options were really doing anything for me in the long run.

A few weeks later, I was looking at my calendar and realized my days were running out. Soon I'd no longer be legally able to drive. So after clearing another half a day on my calendar and putting off other things I wanted to do instead, I wrote the three letters I'd been dreading on one of the date boxes: *DMV.*

Staring at the haunting letters, I recalled the frustration I had every time I'd gone prior and thought, *I refuse to be turned away again.* The eighth trip was going to be different.

I went in the DMV determined to leave as an official Tennessee resident. I had brought tons of paperwork, a full Stanley cup, my laptop to write, multiple pacifiers for my baby, and snacks for mama—I was hunkering down and waiting until someone told me I wouldn't have to come back again.

I was content to wait as long as they'd let me—claiming one of those uncomfy plastic chairs as if my name was on it this time. Wrong paperwork? No problem. I brought backups. Your server is down? No problem. The baby can take a nap while we wait.

I had been discontent previously because the waiting was out of my control and not aligning with my timeline. But when I realized that and prepared myself for the wait, the lack of control no longer controlled my outcome. And thankfully, friends, today my driver's license *does* state that I'm a resident of beautiful Tennessee. If that's not a good time for a little "yeehaw," I don't know what would be!

It's funny that *content* and *contend* are nearly the same word. Some may think being content in singleness is an effortless, easy air you put on, but I believe contentedness is something you contend for—you roll up your sleeves, you pack those snacks, and you say: *No one is raining on my parade today!* Like my DMV fails, it's a lot easier to point the finger at something for our dating woes—to blame the apps, curse the bad dates, and wonder if your soulmate got lost somewhere because of this generation's poor communication style or because another girl "snagged him first"—but we don't find contentedness or clarity by assigning blame; we find it by contending for what we're hoping to find.

Living contently is living in the blessing of hope and casting off the worry of the future.

It can seem foreign to wait patiently while proceeding in prayer earnestly. It reminds me of the ole "pat your head and rub your belly" trick. While not impossible, it does require some brainpower. Our left hand is on one assignment while our right is on another; the same is happening with our hearts and souls in this period. We can accomplish that same simultaneous maneuvering within the praying and waiting—but it, too, will require diligence.

LIES WE TELL OURSELVES IN THE WAITING ROOM

Waiting well doesn't just happen. Doing anything well, especially something we don't *want* to do, requires diligence. It requires diligence, even for the sweetest, most faithful Christians. Loving and trusting Jesus is essential, yes—but it's just the beginning. Even the strongest believers have days where hope feels thin and doubt creeps in. But here's the difference: We don't stay there. The daily renewing of our minds and the cleansing of our hearts—pouring in truth, flushing out lies—keeps us from sinking into discouragement.

Let's pause there. What have you told yourself or believed around waiting? Maybe some of the stories in your head sound like:

- *I'm just not one of the lucky few.*
- *God must be punishing me.*
- *If only I looked like that girl, maybe I would get asked out like she does.*
- *I'm not finding love because I am unlovable.*

Narratives like these quietly chip away at our joy, peace, and hope in seasons of waiting. They aren't harmless, passing thoughts—they are lies. Subtle, convincing lies that slip into our minds and whisper maybe God's goodness has an expiration date, or His silence must mean rejection. They're dangerous to our dating but also to our relationship with the Father. These thoughts don't draw us closer to God—they push us into striving, comparison, and self-doubt.

This is our flesh's attempt to gain control of the narrative by interjecting a false sense of clarity when there is uncertainty. We grasp for answers because waiting feels vulnerable, and we start to think that if we can't find love, then we can at least find a reason for why we haven't found love. Our minds offer up counterfeit reasons that feel like protection but are counterproductive.

But we do not need a solution in a season of waiting; we need refreshing! This is a time to let your roots go deeper in God's presence and to remind your heart that waiting is not a punishment—it's a place where faith matures. It's where God tenderly refines, not because you're broken or behind but because He's growing something that takes time.

Control may soothe the mind, but only God's goodness can refresh the soul.

To know how to be content we must understand what contentment entails, or perhaps what it does not. It does not mean to smile through the pain, deny your desires, or pretend you're pleased when you are not. Being content is being at peace, holding regard for God having you where He believes is best, and being satisfied to the point of not being swayed to settle or drawn to feeling distraught.

Waiting well doesn't mean sitting still, doing nothing, or putting life on hold until someone shows up. It means living with purpose, passion, and faith *while* you wait. It's choosing to grow emotionally, spiritually, and mentally—becoming the kind of person you hope to one day find to share your life with.

For I have learned, in whatever situation I am, to be content. I know how to be brought low, and I know how to abound. In any and every circumstance, I have learned the secret of facing plenty and hunger, abundance and need. I can do all things through him who strengthens me. (Phil. 4:11–13)

IT IS POSSIBLE TO BE GRATEFUL FOR WHERE YOU ARE NOW AND EXPECTANT FOR WHERE YOU WANT TO BE.

It is possible to be grateful for where you are now and expectant for where you want to be. One of the attributes I most admire about King David is his ability to recognize something stirring within his soul and supersede it through lamentation and praise with God. To be raw with where he was, while not letting that be where he stayed.

Are you annoyed at the timeline you're in? Address it with God.

Are you feeling low and lonely in this state? Process aloud with Him.

Are you tempted to settle? Tell God about it.

David knew that anything apart from God is not worth it, and anything with God is never as dark as we may think. He knew that this world, with all its beauty and pain alike, is not our final destination. He experienced exceptional encounters and great grief—love and family, loss and tragedy. David went through times of abundance and times of lack, but what we see through his writing is that God is with us in both—He is our anchor and our answer! "Surely your goodness and love will follow me all the days of my life, and I will dwell in the house of the Lord forever" (Ps. 23:6 niv).

We can adopt that same mantra of contentedness and expectation in our desire for a spouse. And if you're thinking, *Christian, I don't know how to* be *content.* Well, friend, here are some other things you can *be* that will help you develop a content spirit.

Be Joyful

I think many women believe that to be content in singleness you must lose your desire for wanting to be married—as though the only hope for remaining hopeful is setting the bar so low that you cannot be let down. But that's not true at all. You can hold both joy and longing in your hands. You can be deeply grateful for this season while still praying for what's to come. That's not contradiction—that's faith. Being content is to be at rest where you are, even as you dream and pray for the other chapters of your life that are still ahead.

Sometimes joy comes through prayers answered, and other times through navigating pain with a heavenly perspective. Because joy is not happiness—an emotion that arises from laughter and good tidings. Joy is unstealable, significant, and potent for the impact that the Lord provides.

You turned my wailing into dancing; you removed my sackcloth and clothed me with joy, that my heart may sing your praises and not be silent. LORD my God, I will praise you forever (Ps. 30:11–12 NIV).

We can adopt joy even in the waiting because we trust that God is moving on our behalf; we can choose to marry the longing with praise—giving Him praise for all the good He brings (*even if it's still en route*).

Be Believing

Trust that God is at work even before you've seen it. Philippians 4:6–7 directs us in how to present our requests to God: "Do not be anxious about anything, but in everything by prayer and supplication with thanksgiving let your requests be made known to God. And the peace of God, which surpasses all understanding, will guard your hearts and your minds in Christ Jesus."

I don't propose this task is necessarily easy, or we wouldn't need this passage's wisdom and encouragement. But what a testament this model in a woman would be! I imagine this woman who doesn't have the answers, the timeline, or the guarantee, yet her countenance is of someone you'd assume had it all. This pairs well with Proverbs 31—the model of joy on display and faith at work.

Be Present

Being content in singleness means to be at peace with this part of your life and trust that God is guarding and leading you—now *and* later. You don't have to wave a white flag and accept the defeat of your desire. Quite the opposite: I want you to put your boxing gloves on! Get ready to prepare and fight for what you're praying for—not with God, but against doubt, comparison, or anything else that may be stealing your peace. Because what may come in the future is part of the story you're writing today. You cannot rush forward, but you can follow this day's mercy and grace and make it count.

Therefore do not worry about tomorrow, for tomorrow will worry about itself. Each day has enough trouble of its own (Matt. 6:34 NIV*).*

And on the days when waiting is difficult, know that God's goodness does not waver, and His timing is not flawed.

To be a woman who waits well is to believe that even in the silence you are *seen*. That even when your prayers haven't been answered in the way or timing you hoped, God is still writing a beautiful story with your life.

So remember, lovely one, that even in the waiting, God is working on what is becoming. All you have to do right now is simply *be*.

HERE AND NOW

If you find yourself discontent with singleness, you may feel the rush to be married. And that desire to be married isn't wrong. But when longing combines with pressure, urgency, or even anxiety, it makes us feel like we have to make something happen ourselves—and fast. When our hearts are restless, it's easy to fall into unhelpful mindsets or rush into choices we later regret. I'm speaking as someone who's gotten caught in speed traps and dead ends herself, hi!

The truth is, distress isn't a reliable guide. That sense of feeling behind or needing to take control may be a sign that you've begun operating out of the past or living for the future. Let's pump the brakes a little bit. Take a second to just coast. God isn't rushing you. He invites you to breathe, to trust, and to live fully in this season.

While your past is a teacher and your future a vision cast, it's the present that is your gift to actively steward.

The present is the vehicle driving *who* you are and *how* you are. Your past shapes where you don't want to go, and the future impacts who you want to be when you arrive.

Through comments on my podcast, *Dear Future Husband*, and online event forums, I've heard numerous women say that once they get married, they will finally feel complete or all their problems will be solved. And while that longing to be loved and cared for is real and deeply human, I gently want to ask, What does that mindset say about your present self and your future marriage? That you're not enough as you are innately? That your marriage is a Band-Aid to cover something that's broken? Let me remind you: You are not incomplete. You are not a problem waiting to be fixed.

Second Peter 1:3 says Christ has given us *everything we need* for a godly life through our knowledge of Him. While we will have desires, discomforts, and areas of dependence, please know you are not without purpose or provision. You are not in a subclass; you are part of a special class—a royal priesthood—chosen, loved, and set apart in Christ (1 Peter 2:9).

You don't have to be content with being single forever, but I hope you are content with who you are at this present point. Because that version of you will still be with you in your marriage. The image of yourself as a wife is built upon who you are as an individual. It's not a baton pass from season to season but an incremental building. "Single you" matters because she is "married you" too. You're the same person, just with a different last name. So be patient with yourself and be patient in the timing. Because in the same way the extra time at the grocery store picking the ripest fruits and reading the ingredients lists on your snacks makes "future you" feel good and look good, your marriage is going to appreciate that you prepared with wisdom for what's ahead rather than rushing to check out.

If you're struggling to remain content in the season you're in, remember this is a journey, not a sprint. Each season is connected, a step in the same direction and united for the same purpose. Life is full of waiting. Even once you're married, there will still be plenty of things for which you'll have to wait well. So allow this waiting season to teach you the gift of being content in every circumstance in preparation for all the seasons still to come.

DON'T SETTLE

Waiting well means not jumping out of the waiting too early. Also known as: Do not settle!

Chances are we have all invested energy or emotion into pursuing or caring for someone who was not right for us. It could be as innocent as your older brother's cute friend who never noticed you when you were eight or as painful as the guy who didn't respect your boundaries when you were eighteen. But don't let past disappointments convince you to lower the bar. Settling might quiet the ache for a moment, but it always costs more in the end. You are worth waiting for, and the right love won't require you to shrink, compromise your peace, or beg to be chosen.

Settling is never successful.

Now let me be clear: I don't mean "settling" as in don't date a guy unless he looks like a GQ model, has a six-figure income, and greets you with "hello, most beautiful woman in the world" in a rugged Italian accent. What I'm saying is, don't begin a relationship because you're lonely, don't stay in a relationship you do not have peace in, and don't enter a relationship you know would be contradictory to the type of marriage you've been praying for.

Settling is the act of partnering with ill-fit standards or lessening what we accept as love. There could be an awesome guy who's a good friend, but you don't share an excitement or passion with him. A guy who is kind and sincere but doesn't share your conviction of faith and admits he doesn't want to lead spiritually. Or the guy who says he loves the Lord but hasn't submitted his heart to purity to protect you both. Though these types of men are very different, these are all examples of settling.

Precaution from settling isn't rude; it is protective. You're avoiding wasting both of your time by entering into a relationship you know will not be long-lasting. Have you determined what aspect of your marriage would be affected if you settled for subbing necessary qualities in the man you're with? In the example of marrying someone who didn't share your faith, what future obstacles would you face in how you make decisions as partners and parents; or what objections could come to your faith as you decide how to divide your time and efforts? Skimming over important information on commitment and compatibility is settling.

See, the dating period is when we make the most excuses for someone and offer them the most grace. If you already see that you don't share the same values or have concerns about the relationship, these issues will only grow. We don't get an obvious flashing arrow overhead of the man we're supposed to marry when we meet him, but we can see signs if we're supposed to walk away from Mr. Not Right for You.

A phrase my brother-in-law, Addison, often says is, "We allow ourselves to be confused." How a man presents himself to you should give you clarity on where he's headed and what his intentions are. We choose confusion when we blur lines or overlook someone's spoken or unspoken intents and objectives. Maybe you've told yourself things such as, *It's not that big a deal, He didn't really mean that,* or *I can get him to change.* I believe the right man will effectively communicate his goals and vision, but if there's any uncertainty, don't allow confusion—ask.

If someone who doesn't share your morals asks you out, imagine how much harder it will be to settle when you're praying for your future husband and your intimacy to be fortified within your marriage. Even if he's drop-dead gorgeous, you'll remember your invested prayers in your marriage and have to ask yourself, *Is this the man I've been investing in, or am I tempted to settle right now?*

If you've ever dated someone who's unnerved, gaslighted, or ghosted you by making you think you were "too much"—you were too intimidating, you were asking too much of him in your quest for purity, or he was too insecure when others complimented you—this was *not* someone who saw you as a lifelong companion but rather a conquest or competition. To settle for that is an insult to love.

Know who you are and the caliber of love you're willing to partner with. Marriage is a sacred union of two whole people, not two halves trying to complete each other. You have a voice in your future, and you get to choose what kind of relationship you'll build and who you'll build it with. But the clearest way to avoid settling is to be deeply rooted in your identity in Christ first. Because when you know who you are in Him, you won't go searching for your worth in someone else.

I'll be honest—I didn't have a stellar dating track record before I started intentionally praying for my future husband. Before, I was just looking for a cute Christian guy who made me feel pretty and special, and seemed like "marriage material." But what did that even mean for me? What was that material, or substance, that I needed in a marriage partner? It wasn't until I brought it to God in prayer that everything began to shift. My prayers gave me clearer vision, stronger boundaries, and a deeper sense of peace in the waiting. It wasn't about finding the perfect guy to complete the version of me or my future I was hoping for—it was about walking with a perfect God through an imperfect process and learning to trust His timing and His heart for me.

And if you, too, would love to Wite-Out a few pages from your dating log, take heart, my friend. Your past doesn't disqualify you. It doesn't define what you get to hope for, pray for, or believe in. God is not looking at your history—He's focused on your heart, your healing, and your becoming. So don't let shame or regret shrink your prayers. Pay attention to where you're going, not just where you've been. Every prayer you pray now is an investment in your future. And from this point forward, you don't have to waste time settling for less than what God has prepared. Wait on Him and take courage—God (and your future spouse) is worth the wait.

Wait for the L*ORD;*
be strong, and let your heart take courage;
wait for the L*ORD! (Ps. 27:14)*

Praying for your future husband allows you to stop settling because it aids your clarity. We do not pray to God for our future husband in order to *get* a husband, but rather to be *guided* in our heart's quest. For some, you may be guided to your spouse shortly after you begin praying for him. Others may be guided to shift their focus to another area God wants to awaken, such as an initiative or adventure. As we seek Him and seek our desires to be satisfied in Him, one thing is for sure—His timing and direction are always

> WE DO NOT PRAY TO GOD FOR OUR FUTURE HUSBAND IN ORDER TO *GET* A HUSBAND, BUT RATHER TO BE *GUIDED* IN OUR HEART'S QUEST.

trustworthy: "Delight yourself in the LORD, and he will give you the desires of your heart. Commit your way to the LORD; trust in him, and he will act" (Ps. 37:4–5).

How comforting, how beautiful it is to know that we serve a God who doesn't cast aside our deepest cares but acts in accordance with what is best for them. Desires molded with the Lord's instruction produce powerful, protective, and proficient effects.

Your current season isn't a holding pattern; it's a holy assignment. Don't miss the beauty of today while waiting for tomorrow's blessing. Delight in Him *now*—trust that He's not too late, and you're not behind.

Contentment doesn't mean you have to stop desiring—it's believing that where God has you right now is not a mistake. This season matters. He's using it to shape you, steady you, and draw you closer to His heart.

It's okay to admit that waiting can be hard. Especially when you're praying faithfully, watching others step into what *you* hope for, and wondering when it will be your turn. God sees that. He understands the quiet ache and the whispered prayers. And even still, He invites you to find joy *here*—not just when the prayer is answered but while it's still unfolding.

CHAPTER 3

BECAUSE LONGING CAN BE PAINFUL

Here's a reason to pray for your future husband that doesn't take much convincing: because the waiting can be painful. I believe a reader just gave me an "Amen, sister" aloud upon reading those words. That word alone, *waiting*, beckons an eye roll or sigh. Who wants to wait around anyhow?

When I asked a group of single women from our podcast community what they believed to be the toughest part of having faith for a God-led marriage, unanimously it was the waiting. I asked these women to elaborate on how the waiting is difficult, and here's what they had to say:

- "Waiting in my thirties, trying not to lose hope of having a family one day."
- "I find myself doubting if God will actually bring my husband."
- "Trying to not be angry at God for what feels like a delay."
- "Waiting without something concrete or confirmed."

- “Feeling like you’re one of the only ones still waiting while others didn’t have to wait hardly at all.”

I wish I could say the road to love always felt lovely, but that’d be untrue. Sometimes the journey is quick and other times long; for some it’s ease-filled and for others it’s difficult . . . There is no formula.

When I was pregnant with my second child, everyone told me, “Oh, the second birth is always quicker and easier.” I clung to that hope. At first, it seemed true. Labor started and I felt like Wonder Woman—breathing through contractions, laughing between breaks, even dancing and kissing my husband through it all like this was just another date night. I remember thinking, *This is going to be beautiful and quick.*

And then . . . it wasn’t.

Ten hours later—yes, ten—I was still doing all the right things: breathing, praying, staying positive. I even started taking contractions upside down trying to help! But my baby girl? She hadn’t moved an inch. She was high, comfy, and apparently not on the same schedule I was.

I tried to remind myself this was a marathon, not a sprint, and tried to keep my hope in line. The pain was manageable, and I had all I needed around me.

I asked my midwife to check again, sure that we were *finally* progressing. Nope. My daughter hadn’t budged . . . at all. That’s when I started to feel what so many of us do in the waiting: *This isn’t fair. I’ve prayed and prepared. Where’s my breakthrough?*

Sound familiar?

If you’re single and waiting—especially when you’ve been praying and staying true—you know how discouraging it is when nothing seems to shift. You start to doubt the process. Yourself. Maybe even God.

I hit that point where my stamina—physically, but even more mentally—was running out. I looked at my husband and started saying things like, “I can’t do this. This isn’t how it was supposed to be.” Then came a contraction that hit so hard it shattered my hopes.

Seeing my discouragement, my sister-in-law knelt down and gently said, "The hour for a quick labor has passed. Let's focus on what this labor *is*." Sometimes someone we trust calling out our disappointment is just what we need to get out of it.

What I didn't realize was, I was in transition—the most intense, but most purposeful, part of labor. The part right before everything changes. I didn't even consider that an option because the last time we checked, my daughter's position hadn't budged. But when you're praying for something supernatural and special, remember that timelines are never limited.

Twenty-five minutes later, my baby girl was in my arms.

After hours of feeling stuck, it all changed almost instantly. A few pushes, and there she was.

So was the advice about second births being easier true? In some ways, yes. I was more prepared and calmer through most of it. But there were still moments that stretched me, where I had to fight discouragement and trust that God was still working, even when I couldn't see it.

Here's what I learned: Just because it's taking longer doesn't mean it's not working. You're not behind. You're not forgotten. Sometimes the wait gets hardest right before the breakthrough.

So, friend, don't give up! You're closer than you think. There's more occurring at this present moment than you know.

Now, I know you're thinking, *Christian, I need my husband before we start talking about babies.* I know, I know. But I hope this story will inspire three expansive truths about how *you* wait.

1. EVERYTHING CAN CHANGE IN A MOMENT

While you may feel as I did—stuck—it only takes an instant for the next shift to be set in motion. Singleness can be all-encompassing. I get it. It doesn't matter if you've been single for ten months or ten years, stagnant doubt can creep up on anyone—usually due to timelines, expectations, or doubt. For me, it was all of the above. Approaching my literal due date, I became anxious about whether my body would do what it needed to when the time came. Once it did, my expectations for a fast labor overshadowed the good work my body was doing. Then, I allowed doubt to shake my confidence. I wish I had kept confidence in what I knew and remained in faith for what I was working toward. In trying times, it's hard to remember the bigger picture and trust that we won't be in this position forever.

There's a lie we often tell ourselves: The longer we have to remain low—whether in a situation of testing durability such as birth, or a season of testing patience such as singleness—the more strength is stolen from us. But that's simply untrue!

But they who wait for the L*ORD shall renew their strength;*
they shall mount up with wings like eagles;
they shall run and not be weary;
they shall walk and not faint. (Isa. 40:31)

You may meet your husband tomorrow—or you may not. The timeline doesn't matter as much as staying present. I know waiting isn't fun. But when we wait upon the Lord and *with* the Lord, He sustains us and strengthens us. I'd rather work hard and long alongside a perfect mentor and coach such as Christ than quickly and unsteadily by myself. As Isaiah reminds us, His grace is sufficient for carrying us through this season and crafting within us the resilience for the next.

I want you to soar, not scoot; sprint, not slug. I hope you run your race as best as you can, no matter which track you're on right now.

The lie that you're fading in the waiting attempts to steal your speed and endurance. But the truth is that the hard work you put in now, when you think nothing is changing, is actually preparing you for the moment of transitioning from individual to couple. I believe that if I hadn't prepared my body well leading up to birth transition, my body wouldn't have been ready for my daughter to arrive as suddenly as she did. But when we see each time as purposeful and lean into the work set before us, we are better equipped and ready for where He leads. It all can change in a moment, so let's be prepared!

2. WHAT YOU FEED YOUR MIND WILL AFFECT HOW YOU RESPOND

What you say, watch, read—anything that you input into your mind—will affect how you respond to your environment mentally, emotionally, and even physically. There is power in how you speak about this current state. Gut check: Do you say things like, "Everyone is finding someone except me," "I'll never meet anyone," "Waiting around for someone is pointless"?

My fear is that our generation has become skilled at pointing out problems and pain points but forgotten that we can vanquish them. We talk about our issues more than we pray about them and then wonder why nothing changes. Identifying and processing with friends and mentors is beneficial, but if we sense a feeling of being stuck in the same problem, attitude, or situation, then the talking is not aiding us and we're not tapping into healing.

Whenever you're sharing with someone, I want you to ask yourself: *Am I repeating or releasing?* As you confess or communicate a pain point, the Enemy will try to creep in and make it an issue that crushes your well-being and joy—lingering and *repeating* like a broken record, a resounding reminder of what you don't have or can't forget. If you've ever had a circumstance you repeat to everyone, or you find your friend reminding you that you told the same story last week, this may be a repeated narrative, hurting your heart each time you bring it back to the surface. Some phrases common in these habitual traps are: "It's just not fair." "This always happens to me." "I'll never get or be _____." Friend, this is not God's narrative for you.

His approach is the opposite. When we communicate and *release*, we illuminate the truth in the situation and surrender control, shaking off the grip of fear or affliction.

The Word calls God's sons and daughters victorious, declaring us "more than conquerors" (Rom. 8:37). We can confront pain without being confounded by it. I don't want you to fake it till you make it, but I do seek to equip you with a sober mind of resilience, with the ability to identify areas which need healing backed with faith that God is doing just that.

3. SOMETIMES THE PAIN ISN'T TO HURT US BUT TO HELP HEAL US

If we are placing our hearts in the wrong relationships, if we are making a partner our number one over Christ, or if we have places in our hearts that have yet to heal . . . we may feel broken down before we feel whole. Psalm 147:3 says, "[God] heals the brokenhearted and binds up their wounds."

Ecclesiastes 3 reminds us there is a time for everything. A time to weep and a time to laugh; a time to mourn and a time to dance. There are times to tune out the pain and distract yourself, and there's a time to lean into it. Is your distraction aiding you or hurting you more?

I believe God's design for marriage is good, and in His wisdom and grace, His promptings and workings are for our best . . . even if they're painful in the moment. The misalignments of our hearts can be disease-like—leading us to make decisions contrary to what we truly desire for our lives. Part of the gift of singleness, but especially a period of waiting in singleness when you have a desire for marriage, is the chance to invite the Lord in to search your heart and rid anything that is hindering you.

Don't focus on the temporary pain at the risk of missing extraordinary living.

The Bible is full of stories that start with waiting in pain but don't end there. Moses waited forty years in the wilderness of Midian, isolated from his people until the time was right to lead the Israelites to freedom.[1] Jacob worked both literally through the lands and emotionally through the pain of deception until Rachel's father would bless her hand in marriage.[2] David waited fifteen years to take his rightful seat on the throne of Israel while the current king pursued killing him.[3]

No matter how long you've been waiting, how painful some days or past heartbreaks have been, don't give up and don't discredit your journey. God is in the mix.

Of the same women I polled who said that waiting was the hardest part of believing during singleness, they had this to say about what brought them joy and hope while praying with anticipation:

- "My belief that God is capable is my strength!"
- "I get to pray on my future husband's behalf."
- "I know God hears my prayers!"
- "Trusting that all the prayers and time invested are worth it!"
- "Getting to pray rebuilds my faith."

The greatest painful healing story of all is the sacrifice Christ made on the cross. "And going a little farther he fell on his face and prayed, saying, 'My Father, if it be possible, let this cup pass from me; nevertheless, not as I will, but as you will'" (Matt. 26:39). Even knowing this was the intended path for Him, God's best in motion, Jesus still felt all the turmoil and weight of the actions He was carrying out.

As the Bridegroom, Christ gave His all to redeem His bride, the church. We can never repay such a love, but it can teach us about the purpose of a prolonged or painful experience and lead us in our relationships. The pain of waiting on a spouse is but a pinprick in comparison to what Jesus experienced on Golgotha, but we have a Savior who can sympathize with our longings and weaknesses (Heb. 4:15).

Like I cried out for God to deliver and direct me through my labor, I want you to do the same in your longing for a partner—because Jesus is no stranger to the emotions of angst, disappointment, or distress. He is a testimony of the ability to work them toward something greater.

Friend, it's okay to admit if this season has been painful—that doesn't make you weak nor tactless. It makes you a woman who longs for love, walking through the tension that waiting can bring. In this season, tears may fall and frustration may rise. That's okay. Remember, He is near to the brokenhearted!

This is what the Lord, the God of your father David, says: "I have heard your prayer and seen your tears." (2 Kings 20:5 NIV)

Let every tear water the seeds of faith being planted through your prayers. Protect the precious life source that the Lord has given you without building an impenetrable fortress around it. Rather than bury or remain in that tension point, lay it at His feet. Praying for your future husband will help move you from a place of stagnant hope to surrendered trust.

DESIRES AND DELAYS

You may have wondered: *If my desire is to be married, why am I not yet?*

Isn't it wild how quickly our mind can fill blank spaces? At the intersection of desires and delays, our mind generates a plethora of the worst hypotheses for why we're "stuck" here. They commonly take the tone of:

- "It's because I'm not pretty (or smart, friendly, etc.) enough."
- "There are zero good guys left. They're all taken."
- "I missed my only shot at love."
- "I knew I wasn't lovable."
- "God doesn't actually have good things in store for me."
- "God has favorites, and I'm not one of them. He must just love other girls more."

Friend, may I remind you that the Enemy would love to fill your head with ideas that God's plans and creation (you) are ruined, doomed, or forsaken? It's not true. To accurately determine our next steps and not welcome doom in the company of desires and delays, we must fill our blank spaces with God's Word instead of the Enemy's worst.

Let's turn to what the Bible says about the desires and dreams we carry.

Psalm 37:4 tells us, "Delight yourself in the Lord, and he will give you the desires of your heart." The confusion that can arise from this verse is the idea that God freely hands us all the things we want, the notion that perhaps if He doesn't, there's something wrong—with us or with Him. But that's simply not what it means, nor what we need.

A desire is not only a want requested. When we present our asks, needs, hopes, dreams, and cares to God, He refines and reforms our hearts as we delight in Him. This is why we often see David begin a psalm one way (maybe sounding a little whiny, enraged, or a good ole case of hangry), but as he petitions and laments and finds himself in God's presence, his spirit is transformed. God does that: meets us where we are and with what we think we need, as well as how, when, and the way we think we need it. He takes us on a journey to giving, or providing, what we truly need when we truly need it.

The desires God "gives us" are the satisfaction from His providing over and above. Now I'll be the first to say I started praying for my future husband because I was aching to be a wife. God knew my desire was to be married, but His desire for me was to be whole and set apart. Looking back, I can see any delay I thought I was in was actually His protection. It can be hard to realize that in the moment, but the more we remain in Him, the more His presence fills us and all the places in our hearts where desires may not later be fulfilled. The more I found myself in Him, hearing His direction, the more I found myself satisfied in Him.

The more we walk with Him and process what we want and where we're going, the more our hearts are turned to what He knows is best. Our longings become a radio tuned to the frequency of His wisdom.

These longings, along with all other desires in this life, are safe in His leading.

- "In their hearts humans plan their course, but the LORD establishes their steps" (Prov. 16:9 NIV).
- "I will instruct you and teach you in the way you should go; I will counsel you with my loving eye on you" (Ps. 32:8 NIV).
- "Trust in the LORD with all your heart, and do not lean on your own understanding. In all your ways acknowledge him, and he will make straight your paths" (Prov. 3:5–6).
- "The LORD is good to those who wait for him, to the soul who seeks him" (Lam. 3:25).

> THE MORE WE WALK WITH HIM AND PROCESS WHAT WE WANT AND WHERE WE'RE GOING, THE MORE OUR HEART IS TURNED TO WHAT HE KNOWS IS BEST.

In His wisdom, grace, and care, God leads those who are dependent upon Him in His will. Does this mean if you haven't found the one that you're not allowing Him to be Lord of your life? Well, maybe. Surely that's not the answer you wanted to hear, but I have to be honest.

Not having a spouse isn't

necessarily a sign that you're not following God, but it could be a symptom.

Paul was thrown in jail to be wrapped in chains because he *did* follow God, while Jonah was thrown in the belly of a whale to be wrapped in seaweed because he *didn't* follow God. The destination is not how we ascertain whether we're on the right path. Rather, it's being honest in our hearts that we see whether we're walking with God or following our own will—and how much we're letting Him lead and speak.

The woman following God with all her heart and the woman merely going through the motions can both be kept in a season of waiting. I believe delay in meeting our spouse is determined by God. It could be for either intention or protection, or it very well could be because we're not allowing ourselves to be made ready. It's not for us to determine why. But I do want you to ask yourself, *Have I given my all to God?* Not solely your desires but your entire heart?

While we are tackling this section of why to pray, I'd advise each and every one of us to first establish our genuine love and devotion to Christ. As you walk with Him, fully allow Him to be Lord of your life. Then when your spouse does find you, you will be ready to receive him wholeheartedly.

Trusting God, truly trusting Him, means accepting His timing may look different from your own. And it's okay if you have days when trusting feels harder than others—I can assure you that you're not the only one! God is big enough to hold both your hope and your heartache. Maybe the very fact that it's taking *longer* means the foundation is being made *stronger*. Not because you're behind, but because He's building something that will last. Something that isn't rushed or unreliable.

God's not punishing you through delaying your desires—He's preparing you with purpose. This season isn't empty; it's full of enrichment—where trust is deepened, character is refined, and faith becomes real. Keep your eyes on Jesus, not just the outcome. He's not only writing your story—He's walking with you through every line.

I know the waiting can feel heavy—like you're holding your breath while the world moves on around you. But please hear this: God sees you and He has not left you behind; He's right here with you. Invite Him in; take comfort in His presence. This season, as painful or quiet as it can be sometimes, is not wasted.

Keep showing up in your life, even in the in-between. Because one day, maybe sooner than you expect, you'll look back and realize: It wasn't a delay—it was preparation. Rest in the hope that He is transitioning you even before you realize it.

You haven't missed your moment. You're not an afterthought. You are not too late. Because He is right on time!

CHAPTER 4

BECAUSE YOU WANT TO GUARD YOUR HEART

I likely consumed thousands of chemicals in my early childhood.

If you walked into our home on any given weekend, you'd be engulfed by the smell of drugstore hair spray immediately flooding your nostrils. My mother was a Southern mama. This meant she clothed us girls all pretty in pink and painted our toes. She heated our hair in thick curls, then sprayed that White Rain on so heavy that Dolly Parton would have been impressed. Southern mothers follow a secret decree: Dress your daughters perfectly, make sure their bows are never crooked, their hair is never tucked behind their ears, and they never spill their sweet tea on their monogrammed dress.

While I tired of wearing bows the size of a baguette, I loved feeling beautiful and special. My mom didn't just dress us up and teach us to take pride in our appearance for delight. It was often for an event: Whether we were singing at the town's spring festival or being part of the church play, she wanted to shape us to believe in ourselves, to try new things creatively, and to look cute while doing it.

When I entered my first beauty pageant, I was about nine years old. I remember being nervous to take the stage even though I didn't fully understand the premise of the judging. But I smiled once I spotted my family in the crowd. By the time I performed my talent—singing one of my favorite Shania Twain songs—I was having so much fun.

After our performances, I and a handful of other young girls took the stage as our Mary Janes clicked under our flared baby-doll dresses trimmed with ribbons. My nerves returned as they began to announce the winners. "The first runner-up is . . ." I took a big gulp. Then, astonished, I heard my name.

It's me! I grinned just as wide as my tiny cheeks would allow, waving violently at my family in the audience. *They will be so proud!* I thought. But then my glee turned to confusion as I heard the emcee continue, "And the winner is . . ."

Sweet, naive younger me didn't understand that first place and first runner-up weren't the same thing. I thought I had won and felt a quick embarrassment at the reaction my misunderstanding produced. Now, first runner-up in my first pageant was still a sweet victory, but something within me felt swindled because I had briefly experienced the joy of what it felt like to be first place.

I stepped off the stage and was met by my sweet family, who was indeed still proud as I had hoped. But something still seemed off with them . . . *Was the mistake I had made in my mind obvious? Could they tell from their seats that I thought I had won?* Once we got in the car, I realized what had really caused their upset. It turned out that the family whose daughter won had donated the most money to the pageant.

"That's not fair!" "You were robbed!" were some of my family's remarks. I felt comforted that they not only believed in me but wanted to protect me from challenges if they could. That girl could have won fair and square if she was a standout competitor, and something as subjective as a beauty pageant will always leave room for opinions about who should have won. However, if the rumors were true, then I had just had my first experience with a rigged system. Should I have been angry toward my fellow competitor? No, she was just a little girl too! We likely both felt beautiful twirling in our dresses and admiring a shiny little tiara, unaware of the politics potentially occurring behind the scenes. In fact, every little girl who took that stage was talented, beautiful, and admirable in her own right. The problem didn't lie in whether I actually won or not, but in whether I and the other girls had a fair shot at winning.

LOVE IS A BATTLEFIELD, SO WEAR CUTE SHOES

Getting a date itself can almost feel like a pageant—where you have to perfect yourself, stand out, and compete against those around you just to be noticed while someone deserving always gets hurt. If you've ever experienced a bad date, a heart-wrenching breakup, or the feeling when a friend disregards "girl code" and goes after your crush, then I do not have to tell you that our search for love is not exempt from moments of letdown.

What do you do when your heart has been stepped on or left on read? Whenever we find ourselves in a frustrating predicament that seems unfair, the simple response is to take our anger out on the others involved. But the more profitable response is to turn inward and ask ourselves: What can I learn or what can I do differently next time?

Now you don't have to tell me how much you'd rather keep focusing on the delightful part of praying for your future husband rather than venturing to the past or revisiting the hardened parts of your heart. Trust me, girl, I *know* it's lighter and lovelier to lift up prayers asking God to give you a thumbs-up to meet your spouse instead of replaying the times you were turned down or let down. But we must dig there . . .

Why? Because our hearts are incredible organs, capable of restoring and revitalizing not only our bodies but also our minds. However, if there are any residual damaged parts, they can inhibit the beneficial functions of our hearts. We don't want any past pain or problematic ways of thinking to hinder the amount of love we are able to give or the ways through which we express our love to our future spouse.

If you've struck out, been kicked out, or missed out in the past, you could have experienced any of the following: trust issues, fear of rejection, or bitterness. We need to take these out of our hearts before they take us out.

TRUST ISSUES

There could be an entire music genre dedicated to this subject matter. From "You're Not Sorry" by Taylor Swift, "You Give Love a Bad Name" by Bon Jovi, or the straightforward title "Trust Issues" by Drake, there is ballad after ballad recounting a love story gone wrong.[1]

What causes trust issues? Well, they can derive from any trust-stealing injury, like being cheated on, lied to, manipulated, hurt, or let down. They can come from someone you just met or someone you thought you knew. If you have experienced any of those scenarios, I'm so sorry. You didn't deserve to have your trust broken, and it can be so hard to put yourself back out there after being betrayed. It may even be difficult for you to trust God when coming out of a situation like that, much less another human. No one wants or deserves to experience betrayal in what's believed to be a loving relationship. But what do you do after the event to prevent the distrust?

You have to do the work to heal and move forward.

"But Christian, that's not as easy as it sounds!" I understand. There's no delicate way to approach the matter. But let me ask you: What is the alternative? To remain in the pain? No, that simply won't do. See, I believe we're not confined to what we have experienced and God can redeem your love story. But first we must let go of what hasn't served us and what has hurt us, so we can have open hands to receive something new—something far better!

Trust issues can create unforgiveness and fear: two ingredients we don't want cooking in our recipe for a healthy marriage. There's an old idiom, "Don't throw the baby out with the bathwater." In the context of dating, I don't want you to throw out your ability to trust the right man wholeheartedly because you couldn't trust the one before him.

Let me just say it this way: A guy who hurt you has already stolen enough from you in the past. Don't give him the chance to steal from your future!

Many people have a valid reason for trust issues, but what we don't want is the tendency to be drawn toward untrustworthy people. If you bought bad fruit from the same store over and over again, you would change where you shop. Let the same be true for how, where, or why you look for a partner.

Now, I'm aware that trust can be broken by the people who seem trustworthy on paper or come highly esteemed by others. Maybe you were looking in the right places all along and a few of the "good ones" didn't leave you feeling too good. Or you could have trust issues that derive from outside of a romantic relationship—from a family member, loved one, or in the church. This is the most frustrating reality in trust: It can be broken, even in spaces where it was supposed to be protected.

This leads me to think of Jesus—how His chosen disciples, the very men He let into His inner circle of the thousands He could have chosen from, let Him down. In the time of His greatest distress, these men were turning away, turning Him in, or turning up asleep. If I were in Jesus' shoes, I'd have some serious boundaries and walls up after that experience with those closest to me.

But not all hurts are equal. Judas's action of betraying Jesus for monetary gain was a clean break in their relationship, while Peter's abandonment was a temporary pain point. One stepped away while the other came back to pursue. Based on your past experiences and what you currently long for, what should be the standards and boundaries you set in place moving forward?

I'd advise us to be people of firm boundary lines and tender forgiveness.

If someone crosses a hard line or continually fails to support us, that can serve as an expiration date on the relationship. If someone disappoints or offends us, let there be an earnest attempt to gain understanding and get back on track. What we don't want is to lump all mishaps and misunderstandings into a heap of hurts. Heightened trust issues give the people who weren't there for us continued power in our life and steal potential connection from those who want to be there for us.

Working through trust issues is necessary, because even the most amazing spouses will let us down at some point, simply because they're human.

My husband and I do not see eye to eye on everything. Some days I may lose my patience or he may lose his temper, but at the close of each day, we are there for each other, through thick and thin. I do not place my trust in the fact that he will be a perfect husband but that he has committed to being *my* husband. He does not have an expectation that I will always understand him, say the right thing, or meet all his needs. But thankfully he trusted that I meant it when I said I would work diligently at our marriage and continue to grow into the best woman I can be with him. What reconnects us throughout our best and worst days is communication, consideration, and *trust.*

The kind of trust that goes first—offered before it's been proven. The kind that chooses to believe the best instead of waiting for someone to fail. Trust that communicates, "I love you with my whole heart, not just the parts that feel safe." That's the kind of trust we long for in a spouse—and the kind we're called to give. Because love doesn't wait for guarantees; it risks vulnerability for the sake of connection.

So I ask you, will you begin the work of breaking down your trust issues to make space in your heart to give trust to your future partner? Take heart if you're thinking, *I've tried to forget, but my issues still spring up at times.* Your partner will want to hear and learn all about you throughout your time together. He will want to know the areas of your heart to take extra care to protect and nurture, expanding your capacity for healing and allowing trust in him to grow with time.

> LOVE DOESN'T WAIT FOR GUARANTEES; IT RISKS VULNERABILITY FOR THE SAKE OF CONNECTION.

As a future wife praying for a trustworthy husband who wants to give her entire heart to him, I ask you, friend, to take slow breaths and small steps to healing. Protect your heart, but brick by brick, begin removing any walls you have set up. You want to be able to protect yourself while still being able to allow trusted, chosen individuals into the depths of your heart.

FEAR OF REJECTION

No one likes to put their heart on the line only to see the line broken. Whether rejection occurs from a crush or a longtime boyfriend, any instance that leaves us feeling high and dry and wondering if we weren't enough can be hard. But experiencing rejection does not deem you a reject.

Consider rejection a good thing. Yes, a *good* thing! If a man says he can't see himself with you, you should thank him. Take it as honesty, a bullet dodged, or time unwasted. You don't need to be with someone who doesn't have a vision for your life together. Whether it's heart-wrenching or cordial and kind, rejection will serve as protection and redirection. This does not label you as a less-than-desirable woman. Instead, it removes any additional confusion or wrong road from your journey.

I find it interesting that Jesus advised His followers to love everyone (John 13:34) and Paul taught us to be at peace with others as much as we can in our own ability (Rom. 12:18), yet Jesus also assured His disciples that not everyone would like them back (Matt. 10:22).

That kind of prerogative makes you stronger, not bitter. It turns rejection into redirection and heartbreak into holy growth. You may not be everyone's cup of tea, but you'll be *the right* someone's piping-hot chai latte. Rejection is never fun, but it's also never final. Jesus' words still ring true today, even in our dating lives. In a world where feelings often take the lead, what's truly countercultural—and transformational—is letting love lead. Not just any love but *His* love: steady, selfless, and strong. That's the kind of love that shapes us while we wait and sustains us when we're found.

So what do you do after a rejection? You dust off your heart, lift your chin, and keep walking with those cute battlefield shoes. Rejection doesn't rewrite your worth—it simply reroutes your journey. As a daughter of the King, you don't have to chase what doesn't choose you. Instead, you get to trust that God is not only protecting you from the wrong thing but preparing you for the right one. You can bless the ones who walked away, forgive the ones who fumbled your heart, and keep becoming the woman who loves like Jesus . . . even when it's hard. Keep walking, beloved. Your story isn't stuck; it's being sanctified.

REJECTION DOESN'T REWRITE YOUR WORTH—IT SIMPLY REROUTES YOUR JOURNEY.

BITTERNESS

Maybe you're a better human than I am, but every time the Bible mentions some commandment around being unoffendable,[2] the skeptic in me questions, *Really?* When someone cuts you off in traffic or makes an offhanded but hurtful comment, how are you supposed to effectively turn the other cheek? I want to live like Jesus, but how did He do that? (Aside from the fact that He's perfect and all.) Perhaps the more applicable question for this space is, How do you experience pain and heartbreak in relationships without allowing bitterness or offense into your heart?

A breaking of trust or a gut-wrenching rejection would be enough to lead most of us to feel bitter toward the person who wronged us, men in general, or the idea of finding a mate at all. Sadly, it seems like this reaction is quite encouraged in our culture today. As I watched a video clip of randomly selected women my age recount that women don't need men, that men are all trash, or that they hate the opposite sex, I pondered two things: (1) the sorrow I felt for what they have either experienced or been led to believe, and (2) that whether we are single or married, do we want to carry space for that kind of anger?

The misconception of living like Jesus when it comes to offense is the thought that being kind in the face of unkindness is void of pain or emotion. Turning the other cheek is the action chosen, but there can still be other emotions present. We know Jesus felt much of what we have felt: betrayal, sorrow, righteous anger. Yet in each of His actions He conducted Himself in a fruitful manner.

Following a bad breakup, if bitterness is unfruitful, then what action is fruitful for us? Holocaust survivor, author, and evangelist Corrie ten Boom shared how she experienced some of the gravest cruelties in the worst of times yet lived with a heart as light as a feather. After all she experienced and all she was able to forgive and release, she imparted this wisdom: "Forgiveness is the key that unlocks the door of resentment and the handcuffs of hatred. It is a power that breaks the chains of bitterness and the shackles of selfishness."[3]

Maybe you were dumped over text, or maybe someone took advantage of more than just your heart. I cannot tell you forgiveness is easy, but I do know unequivocally that with Christ nothing is impossible. With time, He heals the sting of our wounds—the ones we wanted to simply slap a Band-Aid over to protect ourselves, or the ones buried so deep we weren't sure they could be reached. His love covers all.

The most effective remedy for bitterness is prayer—but it's not always what comes to us naturally.

"Bless those who curse you. Pray for those who hurt you," Luke 6:28 (NLT) tells us. Well, where I come from in Alabama, we're quick to say, "Bless your heart" to someone who's done us wrong, but there isn't much actual blessing behind those words. You're likely well aware of Southern hospitality, but there's also strong Southern sass. It's simply human nature, right? But the fruit of the Spirit is not natural; it's supernatural. Praying will loose the chains from your pain and heal the wounds of your heart. As amazed as I am when I read how unoffendable Jesus was, I'm more amazed to see I can actually follow His example when I am prayerful in a bitter situation. And I believe you can too.

TURNING HEARTBREAK INTO HOLY GROUND

"Create in me a clean heart, O God, and renew a right spirit within me" (Ps. 51:10). I used to read this verse through a shame-splattered lens of Jesus having to do heart surgery on me because of how unlovable I had acted and been—a plea after my worst mistakes for a small hope at becoming that pure and righteous little girl I was supposed to be. But now, after walking with Him for some time (not perfectly, I must add), I see it so differently. This isn't a heart surgery; it's a heart posture. I don't want this to be a Hail Mary; I need it to be a mantra! Every single day you and I need God's grace, and we want to remain as closely aligned to His heart as possible.

As believers, we can give our broken hearts to the One who died for us. He binds our wounds and trades our stress for heavenly peace. There is a time for mourning and grief. Whether you've been hurt, lost a loved one, or feel trapped in a circumstance, you can and should process that pain—but the key is to then release it.

The sentiment that shifted my viewpoint on pain comes from C. S. Lewis's book *The Problem of Pain*. He wrote, "God whispers to us in our pleasures, speaks in our conscience, but shouts in our pains: it is His megaphone to rouse a deaf world."[4] In a world full of distractions and noise, our pain isn't always to our affliction—sometimes it's used to grab our attention. What is God calling you to tend to and why does it need mending?

Our hearts' ability to experience great pain holds an access point to great love.

In love there is great risk, but there's also great reward.

Pain is often seen as our foe, but what if it could be an instructor? The best thing you can do is ask *why*. Why is this painful or why has this pain occurred? Could it be that you let your guard down? Did you lower your standards or lose your way? Or were you hurt or abandoned by someone who should have protected you? This isn't a blame game, trying to shame you for your mistakes or point fingers. This is a chance to assess the damage and cut off its power. The Enemy doesn't care who's at fault as much as he wants those involved to hurt. He sees hurt as an avenue to break us down and break us away from God. However, I believe identifying why we are hurting can help us pinpoint how to heal.

I wanted to journey through these three areas—trust issues, fear of rejection, and bitterness—with you because I desire your heart to be ripe for the fullest love of God and able to love others from that. I may be biased, but I believe my father-in-law, John Bevere, wrote one of the best, if not the best, books on the subject of throwing off our offenses, *The Bait of Satan*. In it he writes, "The focus of offended Christians is inward and introspective. . . . Our energy is consumed with making sure no future injuries will occur. If we don't risk being hurt, we cannot give unconditional love. Unconditional love gives others the *right* to hurt us."[5] I think the Lord is a proud dad when we set aside our reservations—or even our right to be offended—and love despite the risk. But let's be honest: That kind of love takes faith. It's not easy, but He guides us in it. See, God prunes our hearts not to put them in harm's way but to prepare them.

Consider the following Scripture verses:

> "I the LORD search the heart
> and examine the mind,
> to reward each person according to their conduct,
> according to what their deeds deserve." (Jer. 17:10 NIV)

> And without faith it is impossible to please him, for whoever would draw near to God must believe that he exists and that he rewards those who seek him. (Heb. 11:6)

Pairing these verses together, we gather that the Lord rewards those who have faith in Him and walk in His ways, including in forgiveness and steadfastness. The reward or fruits produced by following the Lord are a plethora of never-ending mercies that are not solely the gift of a healthy relationship. Mercies such as these:

- an abundance of grace,
- a surplus of community,
- a pure heart and clear mind,
- the closeness of the Holy Spirit,
- peace and joy,
- discernment and wisdom,
- talent and ability.

The ultimate reward is His presence. When God rewards His daughters, it's so we can glorify Him. And glorying God is loving like Him—unconditionally and counterculturally.

You're not simply "letting people off the hook" when you forgive and forget woes of the heart; you're releasing shackles and receiving so much more.

A BETTER EXCHANGE

Beloved, never avenge yourselves, but leave it to the wrath of God, for it is written, "Vengeance is mine, I will repay, says the Lord." (*Rom. 12:19*)

What we gain when we trade the chance at revenge for the reward of God's giftings is a better foundation for our marriage. Each and every woman who reads this book will enter, or will have entered, her marriage with some type of baggage or wound. But what I'm inviting each of us into is a lightening of the load and a greater exchange. All the fruits and gifts of God are tenfold greater to hold than the chance of being right. And each of His gifts has helped my marriage to grow stronger.

This may all sound fine and dandy in theory, but somewhere deep inside your heart is a faint question of uncertainty. Maybe the trust issues, rejection, and bitterness were not one-off occurrences . . . Maybe they've been the norm for as long as you can remember. I write this with a heavy heart knowing some of you may have hardly a handful of people you can love and rely on. If that's you, I'm so sorry.

When our earthly relationships—with family, friends, or significant others—let us down or sabotage our peace, it can be easy to believe all hope is lost. But I know a Man who will never let you down. No, not your sweet husband you're praying for, as loving a man as he will be. I'm talking about the Man who set out to find and love you before you ever lifted a single prayer: Jesus. He is Abba, the perfect example of love and the One we can forever depend on. He is Jehovah Rapha, the healer who binds broken hearts. He is Elohim, strong and mighty to redeem all that seems broken or lost. Our God alone is worthy of relinquishing unforgiveness and abandoning trust issues, for in Him all the longings of our heart, from now to eternity, are satisfied.

Every person and every relationship are far grander and greater when built upon God's instruction. With prayer as your vehicle, you will navigate the seasons of singleness, dating, engagement, and marriage well. When you pray for those who have hurt you in the past and release them and their action to God, then your gaze becomes more available to see how to pray for your future husband through hope and wholeheartedness.

CHAPTER 5

BECAUSE DATING IS CONFUSING

I detest adding nuts in desserts.

An arguably delicious pan of brownies is ruined when you add nuts to it. Pistachio desserts are all the rage right now, but it doesn't matter what kind it is: cashews, peanuts, pecans—they're all a no for me. They add an unnecessary obstacle that makes it harder to get to the best part—the chocolate! To me, dating is the nuts-in-dessert of relationships—it's a confusing process ultimately inessential to finding your life partner.

Until the early 1900s, "dating" was almost unheard of. Couples largely got to know one another and courted, pursuing each other with romantic interest for a short period of time before making a commitment.[1]

Arden and I met in 2018 and were married in 2018. Yes, you read that correctly, no typos! Though we didn't necessarily plan to fall in love so fast, looking back I can see a few catalysts for our short timeline. It's not often two people get married the same year they meet these days, but it's also no longer common you meet the families on your first date. Our first date was in Florida, where his family vacationed just east of my beach town in Alabama. My mom volunteered to drive me, which I was thrilled about. Then we set off on our day date and went to a local farmers' market, where we "happened" to run into his parents. We still go back and forth with them to this day on whether that was happenstance or subconscious planning. Later in the day, we went back to his parents' vacation spot and played Kan Jam with his brothers. Talk about a family affair!

I never would have guessed my first date with my husband would include my soon-to-be in-laws, but it actually helped us gauge what we were feeling and welcome other trusted voices' input sooner. We had peace, people, and prayer to help aid our clarity without "going nuts" jumping through all the modern-dating hoops.

Countless women have swooned over Mr. Darcy's profession of love to Elizabeth Bennet in *Pride and Prejudice*. While a proposal that raw and eloquent after such brief encounters seems far-fetched by today's love standards, it was the norm for centuries.

People used to know each other for less time before getting married, commit at younger ages, and stay together longer. So what changed? When we replaced traditional courting with the idea of modern dating, much of the process of finding someone and falling in love got, well, *confusing*.

"What's the difference between courting and dating?" you may ask. Courting was more intentional and focused on commitment, and both parties understood the expectations. Today, dating comes with its own subsections and different approaches. I'm not sure anyone can really define *dating* because even those who have dated aren't quite sure how to define it. You can be dating someone but not exclusively or have different goals or timelines than the person you are seeing, while being confused and overattached at the same time.

Some say there's too much flexibility or too many possibilities in modern dating. For example, you can date someone by asking them out in person or by DMing them. You can be girlfriend and boyfriend with someone right away or enter into a situationship without any clear destination. You could date someone for years and call it off in a day.

I asked our *Dear Future Husband* podcast community what frustrations in modern dating leave them exclaiming, "Aw, nuts!" Here are some of their responses:

- "While I'm getting older and ready to settle down, men my age are still figuring their lives out."
- "So many people are emotionally unavailable because of hookup culture."
- "There are *no* good men where I live, especially the ones who claim to be Christian. Or at least, all the good ones are taken already."
- "I see men to meet at church, but they're only meeting girls on dating apps."
- "It's impossible to be the perfect girl he's imagining. One mistake and you're ghosted!"
- "If you meet someone on social media or apps, it's so hard to transition to a serious relationship."
- "The talking stage . . . need I say more?"
- "They *won't* commit."
- "Lack of in-person pursuit at an all-time low. They either won't or don't know how!"
- "Men want a wife and kids but don't want to be a husband or a father."
- "I don't even know how to bring God into dating with how it functions right now."
- "I want to be attracted to the person I'm with, but setting boundaries feels impossible."

What we know as *dating* today is comprised of a gradual taking of marital rewards and responsibilities and bringing them outside commitment. Before, two people would reserve cohabitation, gifting, intimacy, and emotional closeness until they had joined together in matrimony. Nowadays, it's not uncommon for a couple to have been together for years, know nearly everything about one another, and have engaged in various forms of emotional and physical intimacy and *still* be hesitant to put a ring on it. How can that be? Perhaps it's because despite all the confirmation and good vibes we try to gain by experiencing more in the dating period, we cannot bring connection outside its respective realm.

Between the early 1800s and the mid-1900s there was a massive shift in how people found a partner. Courting was the standard for centuries, where potential partners would call upon a woman's family so they could get to know one another. This method was widely led by the parents, in order to find advantageous matches for their children, but it slowly developed into a "calling" method where individuals found someone they were interested in but still kept the evaluation stage around family, community, and accountability.[2]

At the turn of the twentieth century, the origins of "dating" arose, when going on chaperoned outings was the mark of a sought-after woman. These dates were more for social status than finding a partner. Once someone was ready to marry they would utilize the style of courting again. And that brings us to the mid-1900s when war, prohibition, and a handful of other factors invented a closer match to our sense of modern dating.

This is when romance largely went into the hands of individuals themselves. The unspoken narrative was widely understood to be: date *who* you want, which led to dating *how* you want, and quickly turned into doing *whatever* you want when you date.

Today it's estimated that 70 percent of couples live together before getting married, compared to the roughly 11 percent who did the same in 1965–1974.[3] Recent surveys have shown that the marriages of those who cohabitate before engagement were 48 percent more likely to end in divorce than the marriages of those who moved in together after engagement or marriage.[4]

After reading this research and hearing the frustrations from my fellow females and friends, it's clear there is a dumpster fire occurring in modern dating without much intention to put it out. We see the chaos and sometimes feel the repercussions of getting burned, but how do we effectively put the embers to rest? It requires identifying the problem area(s) and inspiring change.

The right things in the wrong timing become the wrong thing.

It doesn't get any clearer, or more blunt, than Proverbs 14:12–13: "There's a way of life that looks harmless enough; look again—it leads straight to hell. Sure, those people appear to be having a good time, but all that laughter will end in heartbreak" (MSG).

In our longing for love, I do not want us to find ourselves lost while looking.

YOU ARE A TREASURE

Marriage is a wonderful gift, but it also comes with its challenges, as every good thing does. Imagine taking a canoe down a river before you received the paddle or taking a walk outside in winter before putting on your coat—the right equipment to navigate the journey and the covering to do it well makes all the difference in how we fare and where we land.

If we choose the pattern of instant gratification over following Christ's wisdom, we're entering the challenges of marriage without its covering.

The old saying "Practice makes perfect" is counterproductive in relationships. Because we don't have to learn love—it is innate. The biblical example of marriage is symbolic of the relationship of Christ and His bride, the church. The more religious experiences we had or gods we loved before finding Christ are not a prerequisite to being a faithful believer.

I believe that as women we are a prize and treasure. A man worthy of beholding and loving a woman should do so keenly. But if we want that type of long-lasting, devoted love, we must take a stand as a group to de-revolutionize how we carry ourselves as women. We can set the stage for love by shutting down what's been shown.

We can be beautiful without having to be admired by multiple men.

We can be sure of our choices without overextending timelines.

We can be unwavering in our desire for clear intentions and expect honest communication.

My hope is to inspire us to live in the hope that good love, and good dating, is possible and to live without compromise until we walk in it ourselves. Pray for your future husband as you desire him to be better than what you see around you. That he *is* a gentleman, that he *will* lead well from the beginning, and that you *are* capable of being a catalyst and component of a new time of dating—oops, I mean courting.

A WORD TO THE WISE

Most weekends I visit my local coffee shop, where I've become a regular. It's dangerously close to my house, and they've gotten the art of coffee perfected. They roast their own beans, make homemade syrups, and have farm-to-table-quality milk. How is my coffee at home supposed to compete with that? (Sorry to my husband and wallet!)

The other day I visited, grabbed my favorite seasonal drink, then sat at my regular table. Between typing breaks and sips, I met a group of women who had been listening to the *Dear Future Husband* podcast on their drive to the coffee shop. We all smiled at our chance run-in, and I got to hear about what they were leaning into with praying for their future husbands and what they were facing as Christian women dating in their thirties.

"There's the tension of wondering when you'll ever meet someone," one started, "while also feeling conflicted when well-meaning family or friends keep pushing options on you that 'should' work simply because someone else is a believer." I nodded in familiarity. Another woman noted, "Then there's the steadfastness you harness to not settle or sabotage purity while you're waiting for the right person to date that butts heads with the anxiety around being unsure of how to even go on a date after you've been single for so long!"

The theme of this conversation? Dating is hard!

I know it can be tough out there. People speak in contradictory riddles:

- "Look with expectation, but don't look too hard."
- "Ask God for your partner, but don't be a complaining single."
- "Try going on a date, but don't date the wrong guy."

I'm aware that the rules and regulations in dating, especially in believers' circles, can often feel confusing or contradictory. Or that even when looking in the right circles, you can still be caught off guard on a date.

But there is a way to connect our praying to our dating—by applying wisdom.

I want you to date like a wise, trained communicator. I want you to know what you seek to get out of dating and to ensure who you're dating aligns with what you've been praying for. A woman on a prayer-led mission for a godly marriage doesn't need to waste her time. I want you to be equipped with wise dating strategies because I don't want you to be blinded or overlook anything important.

Rather than find ourselves confused by modern dating, let's lead with wisdom.

> *Blessed is the one who finds wisdom,*
> *and the one who gets understanding,*
> *for the gain from her is better than gain from silver*
> *and her profit better than gold.* (Prov. 3:13–14)

Let's talk about how to navigate the dating scene while believing for your husband with the following three dating strategies. I believe these ideas will allow you to effectively communicate your goals and ascertain any common ground on dates.

1. Ask the Hard Questions!

When someone first asked my husband how he had confidence in choosing me as his wife, my cheeks turned rosy as I prepared to hear something from a lovesick man out of a novel. I thought he'd say, "Because her beauty brought me to my knees and I was spellbound by the light in her eyes," or maybe something like, "The very thought of her trapped the breath in my lungs unless she was by my side." But his true response made it clear I've read too much Jane Austen. He said the reason he had confidence early was because I wasn't afraid to ask him the hard questions from the start.

From our first date, I tried to probe qualities and answers out of him. I did this because of my dating past when I had fooled myself by believing what I wanted instead of asking what I needed to. I was at a point in my dating journey where I didn't want to play around or waste anyone's time or emotions.

Don't fret; I didn't ask him when he was going to propose or what we were going to name our kids on the first date (though we did name one of our children after where we had our first date). I asked him questions that told me who he was and what he was about.

"Tell me your dreams for the future and ambitions for the next years."

"How important is your faith to you?"

"What do you do for work, and why'd you choose it?"

"Do you like chocolate and dogs?"

The answers to questions like these are telling to a person's nature, and potentially to your future together!

This wasn't typically my style, but my determination to honor myself by knowing who I was giving my time to was endearing to my future husband. If a guy isn't as serious as you are about getting to know you, he's probably only ready to be a boyfriend, not a husband. If you can't be yourself around him, that's not good; and if he does want to step away, let him! You are on a mission to a successful marriage, not safe dating. Ask the questions that allow you to keep taking baby steps toward that goal.

Again, this doesn't mean you need his social security number, ring size, and credit score by the end of the date. However, you should be able to walk away with the assurance that each time you are together you receive a better gauge of his personality, convictions, and vision.

Flirting isn't getting to know each other.

> YOU ARE ON A MISSION TO A SUCCESSFUL MARRIAGE, NOT SAFE DATING.

Small talk isn't telling you much.

Praying for a husband helps you to know what you're looking for, so take initiative from the get-go in figuring out if your date matches up with what you've been praying for.

2. Pay Attention to How He Prepares.

There's a big chunk of wasted real estate in our kitchen: the microwave.

When I was younger, running from school to sports to work, the microwave was a helpful tool to get a warm meal before heading out to the next outing. But after I got married, my husband (bless him) introduced me to a world of wisdom when it comes to healthy eating. (Hey, it's not my fault that I came from the Deep South where everything can be deep-fried, even a Twinkie.)

After I learned that overheating food in the microwave can degrade its nutrients, and prepared foods can be wrapped in harmful containers, I opted to make my food with the oven or stove.[5] Today we hardly use our microwave at all! Because while a food may look complete and delicious, it also needs to be beneficial and nutritious.

Am I going to compare a man to a microwave? You bet I am.

How is he cooking up what he is preparing for marriage? Because a guy may say all the right things, but what is everything else about him telling you? Do his countenance and demeanor match his words? What do his relationships and ambitions say about him? How does he look at you?

I wish it weren't true, but even men who profess to be believers can still behave in a way that doesn't align with their claims. That's why we cannot stop our dating evaluation at mere speech. While it'd be amazing to have a real-life interrogator with you to call out any inconsistencies your date may utter, we don't need a polygraph or body-language expert to be able to determine whether there's consistency in beliefs and actions in someone, because we can follow the Word.

Yes, the Bible can help you spot a player from a potential match. Hebrews 4 shares how: "For the Word of God is living and active, sharper than any two-edged sword, piercing to the division of soul and of spirit, of joints and of marrow, and discerning the thoughts and intentions of the heart" (v. 12).

If he lives the way he says he does, then the fruit will be evident. The Bible is not merely for us to read; it reads us too. Do his life story, his actions, and his behaviors indicate a man activated by the Word of God?

Pay less attention to his words and more attention to his fruit.

This is a useful observation tool because not all ill-matches are bad guys. It's not only the guys with a bad agenda who may not carry the fruit they claim. Some of us want to be a quality partner but have not yet given our full hearts or energy to taking that from a desire to an action. And until we do, we will only be talking the talk and not walking the walk, as they say.

PAY LESS ATTENTION TO HIS WORDS AND MORE ATTENTION TO HIS FRUIT.

The man who is fruitful, not merely hopeful with his beliefs, will have fruits on display—self-control, patience, joy, and more (Gal. 5:22–23).

3. Don't Confuse Good for Godly.

Much of dating is evaluation. You will have to ask yourself, *Is this God's best for me?* You must rely on three things altogether—your prayers, trusted opinions, and Scripture—because one alone can be skewed. If you think this relationship is good but not great, trust that. If you're enjoying a relationship but trusted voices are saying it's no good, trust that.

Don't put yourself in situations, or situationships, that are good but not godly. There's a difference! Just because something can be classified as a *good* option doesn't mean it always will be. And what's good for someone else isn't necessarily *best* for you. There's an element of trust we harness and reservation we relinquish when we ask God to guide us to His best in our relationships.

What does *good* but not *godly* look like? Here are some examples:

1. A comfortable relationship where you get along but that's about all you get out of your connection
2. The "he loves me but not Jesus" relationship where he's a great boyfriend but not part of the Great Commission
3. The too-hot-to-handle relationship where your chemistry is off the charts but it's your sole driving force

Relationships that are good but not godly might feel good in the moment, make sense on paper, or even be applauded by friends—but that doesn't always make them right in God's eyes. We see this clearly in Scripture. Take King Saul, for example: In 1 Samuel 15, God gave him direct instructions to destroy everything after a battle. But Saul kept the best plunder because it seemed *good* to him. He even tried to frame it as an offering to God. But partial obedience is still disobedience—and God rejected Saul as king because of it. What looked good was not *God's best*, and the consequences were significant.

That same principle applies in our relationships. Just because a connection feels *right* doesn't mean it's *righteous*. When we ask God to lead our love lives, we're not just asking for what feels nice—we're surrendering to His wisdom, trusting that His way is better than what looks, feels, or seems good in the moment. What feels good isn't always godly, but what's godly is always good.

So many dating heartaches could be avoided if we paused to ask not just *Is this good?* but *Is this God?* You don't need to settle for what checks boxes when God knows your whole blueprint. There's no power in replaying the past with regret, but there *is* power in reflecting with wisdom—learning what led you off course and what to watch for moving forward. When we know better, we date better. And the best place to gain that wisdom? The Bible.

God's Word isn't outdated; it's deeply relevant, even for our love lives. So let's lean into Scripture, not only for our daily walks but also for our dating journeys. There you will find instruction on how to date with clarity, confidence, and Christ at the center.

GOD IS THE BEST WINGMAN

Too bad the Bible doesn't give us clear instruction for dating, huh? Well, actually, it kinda does! While it may not directly say, "Go here to meet a spouse" or give first-date etiquette and tips, Scripture offers powerful wisdom that can instruct us in dating. How? Because marriage wisdom is dating wisdom, and Scripture has much to say about marriage.

Dating is meant to lay the foundation for a godly marriage, not just fill time or meet emotional needs. We reap in marriage what we sow in dating. So before the vows and the venue, here is some insight that can serve as premarital (or pre-dating) counseling straight from the Word:

- "Let marriage be held in honor among all, and let the marriage bed be undefiled, for God will judge the sexually immoral and adulterous" (Heb. 13:4). This shows us that dating should honor purity.
- "An excellent wife is the crown of her husband, but she who brings shame is like rottenness in his bones" (Prov. 12:4). This verse shows that we should seek spouses, and be spouses, who are honorable in actions and character.
- "Do not be unequally yoked with unbelievers. For what partnership has righteousness with lawlessness? Or what fellowship has light with darkness?" (2 Cor. 6:14). This shows us the importance of mutual faith and mission in who we are relationally tied with.
- "Whoever wants to become great among you must be your servant, and whoever wants to be first must be slave of all. For even the Son of Man did not come to be served, but to serve, and to give his life as a ransom for many" (Mark 10:43–45 NIV). This shows us that love is service. Marriage isn't about who makes you the happiest, but who helps you honor God better together.

When we let Scripture shape how we date, we're better equipped to build something meaningful and lasting. These verses aren't just lofty ideals; they're practical anchors that help us navigate real relationships with wisdom and intention. They remind us dating isn't just about finding someone; it's about becoming someone—a partner. The kind of person who loves well, chooses wisely, and builds a life that reflects God's heart.

Let's heed the relational wisdom the Word offers. As you pray for your future husband, don't just pray he shows up—pray that when he does, you'll recognize him. Pray that you won't trade long-term fruit for short-term feelings. Trust God's timing is worth the wait, and that His best comes without confusion, compromise, or regret, but with clarity and confidence.

CHAPTER 6

BECAUSE IT WILL DETERMINE IF HE'S "THE ONE"

My husband is great at dating.

Wait—*not* like dating other people . . . I mean he's great at making our date nights consistent, fun, and enjoyable. And while he wouldn't say he is the romantic type, he's exceptionally thoughtful when it comes to planning. He can cast a vision, planning something practical yet still special. But back when we were first married, date nights weren't always so smooth. And for one reason—me.

Anytime he'd ask, "Where do you want to eat?" I'd freeze like someone had just asked me to choose the *one* outfit I'd wear for the rest of my life. Suddenly, I was overthinking what sounded good, scrolling through Yelp like it held the secrets of the universe, weighing the pros and cons of tacos versus Thai like my future depended on it. While he's grabbing the car keys, I'm still wondering which outfit to wear and restaurant to choose based on aesthetics and ambience.

Now, sure, careful consideration isn't a bad thing. But when I read the menus of five local places only to pick the first one I'd thought of? Yeah . . . maybe that's a sign I was overthinking it. Thankfully, I've gotten better—or maybe Arden's just gotten better at knowing what I like and planning it before I can start overthinking!

Maybe you're the foodie who sometimes struggles to choose what's for dinner, or the style icon with plenty of options in your closet but who still feels like you have nothing to wear. Or—more likely—you're the woman who's found herself wondering, *How do I know if this guy is the right choice?* Or the single girl praying, *How will I know when the right one actually comes along?*

It's safe to say most, if not all, of us have been there. We don't just want a good choice—we want the *right* one. And when the stakes feel high, we can start playing mental ping-pong with every option. *Is this guy too nice? Too quiet? Too into CrossFit?* We can overthink a single meal, so of course we overthink who we choose to step out of singleness with. Because just like picking a dinner spot, sometimes we're not afraid there's nothing good out there; we're afraid of picking wrong and missing out on something better.

Everyone who wants to get married wants to ensure they're marrying the right person—"the one." This terminology alone can make your palms sweaty. In 2024 there were slightly more than four billion men in the world, making the male species roughly 50.28 percent of the world's population.[1] (Next time you're worried about finding someone, take comfort that there are plenty of male fish in the sea!) How does one find "the one" amid that many possibilities?!

I want you to think of the journey to your spouse less like finding a needle in a haystack or winning the lottery, and more like a trust exercise. Imagine you're playing that blindfold game—you know, the one where one person is blindfolded while walking a path and the other gives verbal directions. Now imagine you're the walker and God's the guide. Instead of looking at all the other options, we can tune out the temptation to go on every date or become overwhelmed by the many choices and instead trust God is leading us on the path He predetermined for us.

Do I believe there is "the one" for everyone? Well, yes, I do. However, I don't think there is only one choice we are allowed. There's more mystery and romance than that! I believe God gives us free choice in all things—our careers, how we dress, and whom we love. But if we want His voice, He will lead and instruct us to the choice that carries His blessing. Then the one we choose becomes the one we are with.

This is where the vision and reality intersect, or conflict. We could call this the Peter Parker predicament or Spider-Man syndrome—you have this heroic image of what your husband will be like, but will you recognize him in real life when he's right in front of you? Spider-Man was idolized by his classmates, but at school they didn't even realize the superhero they talked of so often was a person standing right in front of them—Peter Parker. We can talk, dream, and pray about our husbands to no end, but will we recognize him when he comes?

I want to give you four practical tidbits that, partnered with prayer, will help you determine if a man could be "the one."

1. EVALUATION BEFORE EMOTIONS

Dating is a time for evaluation. But often our feelings and hopes can cloud our judgment. Before emotions are involved, I want you to evaluate this person.

I like to tell my girlfriends to utilize the friend method before their hearts get carried away. Here's how it goes: Remove yourself from the equation. If you weren't interested in this guy, would you recommend him to a friend? Does he have the character of someone you'd set a close friend up with? Does he have any red flags you may overlook for yourself but wouldn't let your friend? We often convince ourselves to bypass any potential hazards in a prospective partner, yet when we are evaluating for a friend, we won't let them come close to settling. I love that we have each other's backs! Let's implement this strategy more keenly for ourselves so we are not leaving our hearts exposed.

Feelings are great, but they should be paired with logic.

I want you to think so highly of the guy you're interested in that you'd be able to give him a glowing recommendation. Regardless of how handsome he is or how fun the first date was, can you allow yourself to step out of the swooning and step into honest assessment?

Maybe it seems a little daunting or disheartening to think about analyzing feelings in dating. I want to assure you that you can date this way and still have fun. This shouldn't be fun-sucking but rather liberating! If you want to bring some zest to this idea of evaluation, let me present this idea: Create a BFFs' BF bingo sheet.

Have a row of green flags you envision for the man worthy of becoming your best friend's boyfriend. Things such as: Does he treat her like a queen, follow through on his words with his actions, and have visible characteristics of God?

When one of you starts getting close to someone, have a girls' night and bring out the bingo card. If the guy passes, "bingo!" Keep going out. If he doesn't, then "thank you, next." These fun girls' nights spent with enjoyment and evaluation will later turn into double dates, then your children's play dates.

2. TRUST YOUR GUT

It's A, no it's C . . . Wait, what if it's B?

Test anxiety is a real problem! Be it elementary school or college, anytime I had to take a test, I was prone to second-guess all my answers.

It didn't matter the subject or question, as soon as I'd circle an answer, I'd ask myself, *Am I 100 percent sure that's right?*

While sometimes rereading the question and slowing down would help me see a point I missed and lead me to a better choice, often I'd just stare at the choices and get them all jumbled in my head. Whenever I was stuck there, I wish I would have *trusted my gut.*

This is a phrase we often use to describe that deep, inner sense of knowing the right choice or direction. It just happens, almost as if we have an inner compass. But whenever we start overthinking, we stop trusting that inner voice. Too much analyzing can lead to procrastination, mental fatigue, or decision paralysis. This isn't reserved for tests in the classroom but can occur when we start to test our relationships too.

So how do you trust your gut when it comes to picking a partner?

I know single people get tired of hearing the phrase "When you know, you know!" Not because it's bad advice—but because it's hard *to know* how to apply it. Women I speak with ask, "What does that actually mean?", "How do I know if I *know,* or if I'm just hoping for this one to work out?" These are valid questions. A more apt phrase might be, "When you know it's a *no,* then you'll know when you *do* know!"

I didn't magically know Arden was the guy for me because I looked into his big green eyes and my heart whispered, *Yay, you've found him!* More accurately, the more I got to know him, the more my heart told me things such as *Wow, I feel safe this time. I'm calm yet excited.*

Honestly, remembering how my past relationships felt wrong showed me that this time I knew something was different. Better. Right.

Take inventory of what is making up your reasoning when you're dating: Who do you get relationship advice from? How much vision for dating and romance do you obtain from entertainment and culture? These are crucial questions to see what we are feeding our minds about relationships. Butterflies are cute, but feeling butterflies is not the only sensation we should have when interacting with our potential mates. We should be able to have that innocent excitement followed by surety. The same way a good meal will leave you full but not queasy, a good date will leave you pleased but not uneasy.

We need to fuel our minds and hearts with God's Word. Renew your mind and let Scripture's wisdom improve your functioning. My true hope is that you trust you *can* have a trustworthy peace in your relationships that is built upon God's promptings.

3. IS HE PURSUING?

Is a man showing you *intention* or *attention*? There's a difference!

I have a friend who is an on-fire, go-getter, young woman of God. She's vibrant, she's beautiful, she's accomplished, and she can't wait to be married. Basically, she's sunshine synced to the Energizer Bunny. Recently she attended a conference with a group of friends and met a swoon-worthy guy: follower of the Lord, hospitable and kind, and easy on the eyes. They had an instant chemistry, and he was respectable and interested the entire time. Yet, after their group hangout he didn't fully initiate asking her out. But he did follow her on social media. Sigh. This is a confusing action (if we can hardly call it that) to decipher.

She wasn't sure what she should do next. Follow him back? Message him? Ask a friend to ask his friend? After some thought, she Instagram messaged him, and they started a conversation. But he still didn't officially ask her out. How could he be messaging her this much and this cheerfully but she still be unsure of what his intentions were? This is when she called me for a coffee hang and brought me up to speed.

Now if you and I are friends, I don't play around with guys messaging my girls. I enter big-sister mode real quick. As she was explaining that they'd been messaging, I didn't ask for a summary; I told her to show me the receipts. Between the blue and white message bubbles, I saw two people flirting but zero clear intention. The farther I went down, the less I recognized my confident, focused, sensible friend in the wording. The woman in these messages seemed unsure and susceptible. The last message she sent was asking him to hang out. I looked up from the phone and saw the woman who had been typing those messages biting her nails, eyebrows turned in uncertainty. "Did I do too much?"

My heart was sad. Not because I thought less of her in any way, but because I thought she was being less of herself. I didn't want someone she dated to get a different version of her. I shared my concerns and said the only thing this guy had proved thus far was that he was good at flirting. I suggested she unsend this invitation to hang out (what an incredible invention, thank you, Instagram) and wait to see if he initiated. She agreed, quickly hit Unsend, and we waited.

I'm glad she recognized desire and confusion were leading her to not be herself and thankful she allowed me to help her process. Because only a week later, she learned one of the friends who had been in the group hangout with them had also been receiving flirty messages from this guy. There was a reason he was showing interest but not initiation.

While you may be confident and a clear communicator, you don't have to force a guy to be clear about his interests. If he's not pursuing you, he is either not the one or not ready to be the one.

I sometimes hear the defense that some guys are shy or the woman is more extroverted. Pursuit doesn't always have to be loud or extreme, but it should always be intentional. Does he make you question? Would progress stop if you didn't keep it going?

Pursuing can be complex because of personality types and cultural differences. While one man's pursuit may consist of asking a woman out on a date upon first meeting and showing chivalric romance from day one, another's might involve attentive conversation and a gradual increase in closeness. Regardless, three things should ring true in any man's effort—honesty, openness, and intention.

Now let me be real for a moment: I hear you—the woman reading this from a small town in Idaho, thinking, *The dating pool would be better if I lived in Nashville or New York.* And hey, I get it. Bigger cities often mean more options. But more options don't always mean better outcomes. I've seen plenty of women in places buzzing with singles, or who have that look or personality men gravitate toward, still wrestling with the same core issue: *Where are the men who actually know how to lead well?*

Because here's the truth: If a man is called to lead, he must first *be* a leader. And leaders aren't defined by zip codes, follower counts, or fashion sense. Real leadership comes in all shapes, strengths, and stories.

As you pray for your future husband, ask God to reveal to you who *you* are more clearly—your giftings, your values, your vision—so that when someone steps into your life, you'll be able to discern if he's merely someone with potential or a potential partner for you. A powerful question to ask early on is: *Can I see this man as a leader whose vision I'd be honored to complement and build alongside?*

Love isn't supposed to feel like a roller coaster—flying high one minute, then questioning all your life choices with your hair a mess and your heart in your throat the next. No thanks. Real love is better equated to a sailboat ride—smooth, steady, and headed somewhere on purpose. Sure, there might be a little wind and waves, but you're not white-knuckling your way through it. Let's stop bracing for the drop and start looking forward to the view. In genuine love, we can be anchored in peace, move forward with confidence, and set our sails on a hope-filled future.

Love is patient, love is kind. . . . It always protects, always trusts, always hopes, always perseveres. (1 Cor. 13:4, 7 NIV)

Rest in the peace that God's timing isn't rushed by circumstances, location, or comparison. Yes, pray for a man who can lead with intention. But more than that, pray that *you* will be led by peace. That when love comes, it won't confuse you—it'll *confirm* everything God has *already* planted in your heart.

4. BRING GOD IN FROM THE BEGINNING

I love that we women have our own codes and languages only we can decipher.

If our man or roommates are out of town, that means we're having girl dinner: a slice of peanut butter toast, bowl of cereal, or crackers with cheese. If we are meeting friends for an event, it's common girl knowledge you have to ask for the dress code. "Cute or casual?" I've sent that text more times than I can count. What would happen if my friend didn't reply in a timely fashion, though? If I thought grabbing a coffee meant sitting at a table and hanging out for a while, but she thought it meant grabbing it and going on a brisk walk to get our steps in? If she waited to text me back and let me in on the plan until after I'd left the house, then I'd show up in low heels and a dress while she came in her Lululemons and sneakers.

If we want our plans to go a certain way, it works best to prepare ahead of time.

Similarly, don't wait until your wedding day to bring God into your relationship. We can't pull that late move and text God, "Hey, I'm already on my way down the aisle, but meet us there!" Bring Him into your relationship from the beginning. Be on the same page with God before you let another into your heart. After all, it's common courtesy: God was there first; this guy on the date is the newbie!

In the same way we girls want to align our outfits with our friends, we also want to align our steps with God's guidance, as daughters guarding our hearts and honoring what He has deposited into us.

The Lord *directs the steps of the godly.*
He delights in every detail of their lives. (*Ps.* 37:23 *NLT*)

Ask God for direction with each progression of your relationship, and ensure that this man has a relationship with Christ. Does he treat others in a biblical way, or does he bad-mouth or gossip? Does he attend church and engage in prayer regularly or does he seem to be too busy? To be a good leader, a man must first be led himself. Does he pray for vision in your relationship? Does he honor Scripture and virtue? Seek out and depend on this! His heart for the Lord should be even more evident than his heart for you.

A godly husband loves God more than he loves you, which enables him to love you well.

A GODLY HUSBAND LOVES GOD MORE THAN HE LOVES YOU, WHICH ENABLES HIM TO LOVE YOU WELL.

Your spouse is the second-most important and impactful relationship you will have in your life, behind your relationship with the Creator. Our desire for romance cannot trump or supersede our first love. And when our romantic relationship follows God's model and aligns to its instruction, then we find the blessing and benefit that allows for a thriving union.

To close out this chapter, I want to share four practical signs that a guy could be "the one":

1. *He will aid your peace, not add confusion.*
2. *He will treat you with integrity and respect your vision.*

3. *He will be someone you can trust wholeheartedly.*
4. *He will love God even more than he loves you.*

If you want to find "the one," start by finding Jesus and being found in Him. Of all the wisdom and advice you can receive from family or mentors, no earthly words can match the divine instruction from God. For any route we journey in this life, let's bring God in before we start stepping. If we want to hear His voice, we must start listening to Him.

CHAPTER 7

BECAUSE THERE IS BLESSING IN THE CHOICE

There you were: sitting at a family friend's or relative's house, minding your own business and playing politely, when an adult with a super-friendly smile leaned over, casting a shadow over your toy, and asked, "What do you want to be when you grow up?"

Some of us have known the answer to that question since we still had training wheels and handle ribbons on our bikes, while others of us are *still* trying to answer that question. How's a little girl with Velcro shoelaces and mismatched-dressed Barbies supposed to confidently know what career she wants to choose?

For years my own answer was a fashion designer. Preferably I'd have a studio in Paris making couture pieces and mesmerizing footwear. This idea lasted long enough for me to aspire to attend FIT, the Fashion Institute of Technology, in New York for school. But the more I studied the classes and expectations of such a career, the less I felt it aligned with me. I wanted to be creative but felt my love for fashion was more an appreciation and that I lacked the innovation required. The students I'd see in fashion school made every hallway a runway, debuting outfits they had crafted by hand, fashioned in ways I never would have imagined.

Now, I no longer dress Barbies, and I set aside my previous dream of designing dresses, but I get the honor of creating resources, both in written books and online podcasts, that have connected me with incredible women like you. (Oh, and I also get to be my husband's stylist!)

So how do you have confidence in your choice in a spouse if other important choices, like your career or goals, mature and change as you do? How do you know which desires and decisions are the right ones to lean into?

God has fashioned someone uniquely aligned for you.

Similar to my discovery when I did a deep dive into the fashion world, I believe pairing your desires with wisdom and evaluation will allow you to have confidence in your choice for a spouse.

WHERE ART THOU, ROMEO?

Finding "the one" can sound romantic in fiction but daunting in real life. In a literary flip of fate, Laurie and Amy from *Little Women* found a later-blossoming love. Even in a family feud where love was off-limits, Romeo found his love, Juliet. What was their secret?

The secret to finding "the one" is to make the evaluation serious and the choice peaceful. This flips modern dating on its head. While dating starts casual, then gets confusing in taking the next steps, this approach allows us to get serious with God first before we misstep.

I had dated both well and poorly in my single days, good guys and should-have-known-better guys. And I made a mess of both. No matter how happy or confident I started any relationship, eventually it'd fall apart, and I did not like cleaning up the mess.

The day Arden first reached out to me, I realized this man was a true contender, the standard I'd been praying for. I threw (yes, legitimately threw) my phone in the back of my car and said, "Lord, don't play with me. I cannot mess this one up. This is a good guy. I'll only move forward if he is the one!"

Looking back now, that was a rather hefty ultimatum to place on God. Yet my aim wasn't to test God or get my way in my timing. I knew how much God had healed my mindset, and I didn't want to fall back into past patterns and mess up another relationship, especially with a good guy. I knew I needed God's direction and clarity.

There is a blessing that rests on us when our choice is founded in Christ's direction and we are certain with our whole heart.

Your choice makes your spouse the one.

Not your ability to pick the perfect person or to be lucky in the draw. It takes initial effort to determine where you're going and if this person is on mission with you, then consistent effort to draw together throughout that journey. Those two alignments allow you to be with "the one."

How do you find a spouse, though? You can meet people at school or church, on social media or dating apps, and through family, friends, or work. We have more access to others than ever, yet many feel all the less known or connected, particularly due to the expansion of social media. Researchers are divided over whether its creation has been overwhelmingly good or bad, with both sides presenting strong arguments.[1] However, many agree it's hindered interpersonal skills and our ability to relate to one another.

No doubt this has bled into our dating. Maybe you're surrounded by people but have not found any promising potential dates. Or you can connect with and follow a variety of guys online, but how do you know who would really be a good guy to date? Sure, there are tons of fish in the sea, but dating in this social climate can feel like you're floating adrift in the ocean on a tiny inflatable.

There's a common FOMO approach that can affect dating and haunt our choices. Nearly every person has worried they might choose the *wrong* one. Well, it's not a matter of *if* you'll choose wrong but *when.*

Let me explain.

FOMO is a real diagnosis for our generation, as there are so many people in the world and so many ways and places to meet them. Whomever you choose will feel like the best choice some days and the wrong choice on others. That's why you have to trust your choice when you make it. Whomever you find, wherever you find them, you choose to make them "the one" every day.

My husband and I have committed to strive to be the best partners we can—in connection, in family life, and in ministry. We serve one another's needs to the best of our ability. But my husband will never have or be all I want, and neither will I be all he wants. Because wants aren't stable. They can change with the season and perception. If my husband suddenly wanted a wife who could cook like Julia Child, I could not satisfy that want. But he doesn't *need* me to make gourmet breakfasts, lunches, and dinners; he just needs me to look out for our family's well-being. Likewise, if I decided that as I became more creative, I wanted a spouse who was equally artsy and could paint stunning portraits or write songs about me, my husband couldn't fulfill that want. But my *need* is support from my partner in my ventures, and he fulfills that need well.

After the honeymoon phase, you move past initial romance and into real relationship. Don't panic! There are still plenty of sweet smooches and butterflies ahead, but something deeper and foundational forms after you move past the "happily ever after" mindset and into the "he's my guy for life" partnership-building stage.

This is a good thing. Because it's when the rubber meets the road, when we really hit conflict and real life with our partner, that we are truly able to begin building together. The challenge we face is leaning away from the "what-ifs" and leaning into the "what cans." What can we learn from this obstacle? What can we overcome together? What can I do to continue making him "the one" through how I think, speak, and act?

Commit your way to the L*ORD;*
trust in him, and he will act. (Ps. 37:5)

When it comes to marriage, I have to believe when we are fully trusting in God's paths and asking Him to lead us in our relationship, then He will be with us in our decisions.

I sure do feel lucky to have found my husband, but I do not believe "luck" had anything to do with it. See, you don't have to be perfect, calculated, or superstitious to find your husband; but I believe we should be submitted. Because if we want to find a partner and enter a God-honoring marriage, the surest way to find that course is through submitting to God's ways and plan. God works all things out for our good when we believe Him and permit Him His rightful position as Lord in our life (Rom. 8:28).

In the end, the goal isn't just to find a man—it's to be found in Christ. He is where your worth, wisdom, and direction (for yourself as an individual and your strength in your relationship) begin.

SHOULD I HAVE A CHECKLIST?

Which type of vacation packer are you: a type A itinerary queen with preplanned outfits for each day and event? (Fellow over-organizers, hi, how are ya?) Or are you the "throw it in the bag and hope for the best" kind of gal, relying on the powers of dry shampoo, one maxi dress, and your black Lululemon leggings you'll end up in 99.9 percent of the time?

Whether you're traveling to a tropical beach or bundling up for the Swiss Alps, you pack based on where you're going—not just what you feel like wearing that day. As easy as it'd be to toss in whatever's cute or convenient, wise travelers think ahead. They plan with purpose. And this is even *more* true in dating.

Marriage isn't some spontaneous weekend getaway—it's more like a lifelong road trip with someone who will see you without makeup, moody, and at every emotional pit stop along the way. If your copilot is cute, that's great, but compatibility, shared vision, and spiritual alignment are what's essential.

So before you start swooning over the guy in your DMs who has great hair and a golden retriever, you have to ask: Does this person have what it takes for where I'm going? Are we headed in the same direction or am I trying to pack beachwear for a blizzard?

Let's unpack (pun intended) how to have a *righteous* checklist.

Some women have been told having a list or type in dating is too picky or overly critical. When it comes to choosing our spouse, I believe it's beneficial to know if we are making a good choice or not, and knowing what we are looking for in a spouse can help determine that.

We date differently when we know what we are looking for, and prayer sets the stage for the believer. Prayer is more than a request; it is a powerful communication with the One who knows all and knows best. As Pastor Henry T. Blackaby said, "Prayer is not a one-way conversation where you simply recite everything you want God to do for you. It is two-way fellowship and communication. . . . Prayer also includes listening. In fact, what God says to you in prayer is far more important than what you say to Him. . . . Through prayer, you adjust to God; God doesn't adjust to you."[2]

What may God be saying to you about your future marriage, and, even more specifically, about your future husband?

From a young age, many of us began envisioning what our future husband would be like—his personality, looks, interests. "Dreamy" was on the initial checklist, no doubt. I'm sure a few other phrases that spanned those early checklists were:

WE DATE DIFFERENTLY WHEN WE KNOW WHAT WE ARE LOOKING FOR, AND PRAYER SETS THE STAGE FOR THE BELIEVER.

- Tall, dark, and handsome
- Romantic
- Kind
- Man of faith
- A chivalrous gentleman
- Athletic and fit

Is there anything wrong with this list? I don't believe so. But are these Spirit-led or world-led attributes?

I see lists as beneficial. You are developing for the season ahead, wanting to be intentional in your looking for your spouse. However, the error lies in when we are ruled by our ideas more than moved by the Spirit.

As avid Pinterest users and dream-board makers, we are visionaries who like to have direction and a keen picture of the finished product. Personally, my guilty scrolling pleasure is browsing idyllic houses and amazing architecture. I'm the girl who hunts on Zillow when we're not even thinking about moving. But how does one make a dream house? What lies within the walls of those gorgeous homes?

As much as I love Pinterest, it can be easy to forget the steps and grit it takes to build something beautiful when staring only at finished products. On the app, we see the beauty and outer materials. But only those involved in its making saw the concrete in the foundation, the pine in the frame, and the piping for the water. There is more to add to a building checklist than the outer materials, which are nothing without the foundation. The same is true for your checklist for your spouse and marriage.

When praying for your future spouse, God will illuminate big and small things for you—important criteria to put on your checklist before dating someone. In a new build, the architect brings understanding of the configurations and scope while a general contractor knows the building codes and specifications. In a new relationship, the Word brings you confidence and scriptures while the Holy Spirit gives you clarity and guidance.

When you develop a checklist for choosing your future spouse, and hold it loosely while being led by wisdom, it can be a beneficial device in your decision-making.

"So you're saying to have a list . . . but don't bank on it? Ugh, wouldn't it just be easier to throw it all out and have no list at all?" Sure, that'd be easier. I remember a sermon going viral a few years back advising people to ditch their lists in dating.[3] And while I appreciated the fundamentals of the message—suggesting that dating shouldn't be superficial or uninspired—I wasn't sure if I'd come to the same conclusion. Because while we don't want to make traits of our own advisement absolute if they lead us into vanity or complicate the process, we also don't want to date unexpectedly or unadvisedly.

My advice is to make your checklist, but build it upon what matters. When you look at your checklist, evaluate it through the following criteria:

1. **Absolute and concrete:** These are the non-negotiables you need to see in dating before getting serious about marriage. For example: having shared faith, wanting children, being hardworking. These are the areas that don't magically appear or change after you say "I do." What are the most important things in your life or your greatest desires for the future? Those should lead what you put down for absolutes in your future spouse. To be in an iron-sharpening-iron, Christian relationship, you'd seek someone who's committed to that refinement. And yes, it's okay to have non-negotiables! Not everyone will

adhere to or agree with what's indispensable in your life, but the person who becomes your partner should.

2. **Hopeful yet flexible:** These are desires close to your heart, but they don't have to unfold *exactly* how you've imagined. Longing for a partner who loves people, communicates well, and shares mutual attraction is valid. But perhaps how those qualities show up might look a little different than you pictured. This doesn't suggest lowering your standards; it's about holding your vision with both hope and flexibility. For example, maybe you've always dreamed of being a missionary overseas, and you've prayed for someone with that same calling. That's a beautiful desire! But what if God calls you and your future spouse to a slightly different mission—like serving as inner-city counselors or discipling college students in your own community? The heart of the calling is still there, even if the zip code requires a bus pass instead of a passport. Or maybe attraction looks different than you expected. You thought he'd look like Chris Hemsworth, but he's more of a Chris Pratt—brunette instead of blond, with humor, kindness, and the type of smile that grows on you more each day. The core of these desires can remain the same, but the details can shift. Trust God sees the full picture and knows just how to weave it together in a way that's even better than your checklist. What's important for these areas is that the heart of the matter remains the same but the outworkings and details can be different.
3. **Non-impactful:** Any item that is of little importance to your relationship or too detailed to be influential. These are often socially influenced. For example: "Must be over six feet tall, love cats, and come from a big family." Would you really turn someone away for being five foot eleven, having a preference for dogs, or loving his family well but being an only child? While innocent, items like this can waste our time or get in the way of

evaluating the pieces that truly matter. These are either trivial or work themselves out later. Maybe you end up loving him being a little closer to eye level for kisses, you get a dog and a cat, and he becomes best friends with your many siblings while his parents feel like your bonus parents. There are so many rivers we cross once we're married; don't let the little things become big things.

I encourage you to write out all the particulars you desire in a spouse and mark them as one of the three criteria. Keep all the ones, loosely hold the twos, and cross out the threes.

The Bible says "we know in part and we prophesy in part" (1 Cor. 13:9). I believe that as we earnestly strive to walk in the path God has called us to and search for the person He's designed us to walk alongside, He will give us what we need to know about our partner and keep some parts for us to discover.

Your standards should be based on principle rather than profit. Standards are not certain heights, bank statements, or crafty compliments. Standards are moral guidelines, deal breakers, and vision.

Here are my boiled-down thoughts on having a checklist for your husband: Lean into what God places on your heart and leave the specifics to Him. There are attributes of your husband you will prayerfully look for, and others God may reveal to you when you meet your husband in real time. Let it be a mystery; allow some wonder to remain! Share your list with God and allow Him into the evaluation process with you. I cannot think of a more trustworthy consultant.

EENY, MEENY, MINY, MOE

Has anyone ever asked you, "Why are you still single?" Or perhaps they, or you, assumed if you're a Christian going to church and desire to be married, there should be virtually no issue checking that box. I, too, once thought it should be that simple.

In my early twenties I joined a church internship with a group of incredible peers and leaders. The kind of people you really could hang out with every day. Which is good because we nearly did. We'd set up and tear down together, host small groups, and then continue enjoying our free time together, usually at whatever food establishment our broke-college-kid budgets allowed for.

We were encouraged to not date during the program but nonetheless were given random love advice from time to time. I still remember when one of our leaders told us the solution to finding our mate: "All you have to do is find someone who loves Jesus and that you're attracted to."

Wait, that's it? As much as I'd hoped it really was that simple, something about the statement instantly didn't sit right with me. Surely there has to be more to the equation or else people would find a partner with much more ease and more marriages would last. I appreciate what he was trying to do: add ease in an area filled with confusion and corruption. However, to say any good Christian guy and any good Christian girl can link up feels, well, insufficient. To say any ole one would work means that everyone would work, and what's the point of being paired if everyone is interchangeable?

The point was to seek someone who loves the Lord above all and with whom you share a genuine connection—but it's no magic formula or two-step process.

Selecting a partner is more than a game of eeny, meeny, miny, moe.

I don't believe everyone with a voice can be an excellent singer. Or that everyone with two feet can be a skilled soccer player. Likewise, not everyone with a good heart can be a potential match. In all these areas, there's more than the mere sum of parts that make for something strong, skilled, and sure.

I also like to imagine God is like a Michelin-star chef—creating the best concoctions from a variety of ingredients that make for delicious plates. Gordon Ramsay is famous for his beef Wellington, which sounds delicious, but after looking at his recipe, I never would have thought to brush beef with mustard and horseradish, then top it with ham and mushrooms—or that I'd enjoy the combo. But that's why he's the famed chef, not I! He knows the ingredients that go together and the zest the right abundance can bring.

I think God, too, sees a variety in you and your partner and what will pair well together. It's more than just the steak and potatoes on a praiseworthy dish; the seasoning, the marinade, and the toppings all play into the overall experience. While faith and looks are very important to the harmony and longevity of a relationship, we need to bring more into the kitchen of evaluation.

This two-ingredient advice I heard lacked romance, deeper thought, and intentionality. As significant as your choice of a partner is, you don't want it to be a shot in the dark. You want to be guided by the light!

"I am the light of the world. Whoever follows me will not walk in darkness, but will have the light of life." (John 8:12)

Jesus set the example of trusting in the Lord in all things. In how we act, the way we treat others, even what we eat—glorifying God through it all (1 Cor. 10:31). If we want to have marriages that glorify God, I believe we should be led by His light. That is how you choose in peace—with guidance. Then on the hard days, you won't look back with regret but with reassurance. And on the best days, you won't gloat thinking you've got it all figured out, but will hold gratitude for what He has done through and within you both.

"Blessed is she who has believed that the Lord would fulfill his promises to her!" (Luke 1:45 NIV*).*

There is blessing with your choice of a spouse; and there is a holy guide who stands near us in our free choice and aids us with wisdom throughout. You don't have to figure it out alone. You don't have to settle just because time is passing. You get to choose—and God will aid you in your decision.

THERE IS BLESSING WITH YOUR CHOICE OF A SPOUSE; AND THERE IS A HOLY GUIDE WHO STANDS NEAR US IN OUR FREE CHOICE AND AIDS US WITH WISDOM THROUGHOUT.

You are not powerless in the waiting; you are empowered. He empowers you to choose with clarity, not fear—to have a love that not only *sounds* good but is also good *for your purpose.*

CHAPTER 8

BECAUSE COMPARISON IS REAL

Growing up on the Gulf Coast of Alabama, I was raised knowing how to respond to a hurricane threat. Where we lived, right near the Alabama-Florida line, we'd experience roughly seven hurricanes a year, so it was important to know what to do so you could act quickly if need be: Keep a generator on standby, have plenty of water and shelf-stable foods, board up the windows if you didn't evacuate, and as tempting as it is to go play outside when the weather appears to clear, don't, because the eye of the storm is a false and fleeting time of peace. The few large hurricanes my family rode out, we followed these guidelines and made sure we were positioned to stay safe in our home during the inclement weather.

Having this problem-solving knowledge was greatly beneficial when a natural-disaster threat arose. But during the pandemic in 2020, I was surprised to see a different type of rationing occurring. When I made my way to our local grocery store in Colorado, I was shocked to see the shelves emptied not of water, nor food, but of toilet paper.

What's now laughably called the Toilet Paper Pandemic shows how a scarcity mindset can lead us to overbuy any supply we think may be limited. Stores had to limit how many packs a family could purchase at checkout because some customers were buying two or three times the amount they could possibly need. These panic purchases shifted the way customers interacted with suppliers and other consumers. And while I'm thankful for toilet paper and for us to have proper bathroom etiquette, I can't help but think how we can feed that same panic mentality when we think supply is limited in the dating department.

No one tells you that during singleness you'll have to face off with the scarcity mindset—which is filtering life through the lens of what we don't have and believing there's only so much of it to go around. This is a way of thinking that breeds angst in our approach to dating. We become like a crowd of Black Friday shoppers, bumping shoulders with the women on our left and right, hoping they don't beat us to the item we're eyeing.

When we see love through a lens of scarcity, we begin to view other women as competitors and men as trophies—losing sight of the true value in both. The more this view plagues our thinking, the more comparison arises in our hearts. It's almost as if we believe the journey of finding a spouse is a race that has inevitable losers, and we don't want to be one of them. Whenever we see another woman happily engaged, our flesh can cry out, *Great, one less option for me.*

This isn't a new challenge reserved only for our toilet-paper-hoarder generation either; it's been common for centuries. The famous phrase "All is fair in love and war" can be traced back hundreds of years,[1] yet that feeling still lingers today, doesn't it? Sometimes we're tempted to see other women as competitors or opponents to our own marital happiness. But I'm of the belief that if something is for me and I'm living in a way to receive it, it can't be stolen. I also can't picture our God, who is righteous and kind, setting a man out for two women to fight over. "Put your boxing gloves on, ladies; who's going to get him?!" That's simply not His nature. You're not fighting other women for a man; you're fighting for *your* marriage! So let's not treat men like toilet paper—your chance for love isn't flying off the shelf.

BUT I'M OF THE BELIEF THAT IF SOMETHING IS FOR ME AND I'M LIVING IN A WAY TO RECEIVE IT, IT CAN'T BE STOLEN.

THE JOY ROBBER

Comparison will rob you of joy—not because another person can steal it from you, but rather because scarcity thinking squanders our opportunity to realize and receive joy. Jealousy is infectious. It will cause us to be skeptical of those around us, ourselves, and even our Creator.

More than once, I've read through comments of women in reply to an advice-driven post that they don't want to hear from a married woman. I translate this as "You don't get what I'm feeling" or "You got out of the pain so don't talk to me about mine."

The Enemy's strategies are laced with undertones; they're never fully what they seem on the surface. So when it feels like no one understands you and you want to push everyone away, that's the Enemy trying to isolate you, to weave in shame and shut out hope. If you feel hope draining from you and you ask how God could do this or that to you, that's the Enemy trying to turn your eyes away from faith and the hope in your future.

Be sober-minded; be watchful. Your adversary the devil prowls around like a roaring lion, seeking someone to devour. Resist him, firm in your faith. (1 Peter 5:8–9)

If you're in a season that feels overwhelming or discouraging, I implore you to seek the Word's guidance for belief and encouragement. The Enemy's subtle suggestions will be actions that isolate, discourage, and belittle you. But Scripture tells us to speak life into our doubts (Isa. 55:11), immerse ourselves in God's presence and practices (1 Tim. 4:15), and find support in community (Gal. 6:2). You do not have to walk this alone, and I daresay when you feel alone is the time you most need to seek those who are committed to walking with you.

In the waiting, isolation and doubt can become building blocks for comparison. And wouldn't the Enemy love to see us on our own when we're in our heads? Isolation whispers, *Push them away; they don't get it.* Doubt mocks, *They took the last good guy, nothing left for you.* Even when we are surrounded by great friends and loving family, comparison can slowly work a wedge into our thinking.

It happens more often than you or I would like to admit: when your best friend FaceTimes you to flash her new 1.5-carat engagement ring while you're still mourning a recent breakup, or when your sister is going out on a date while you're sitting at home on a Saturday night. I've been there too. But we have to remember there is no fixed timeline in love—everyone's seasons begin and shift at different paces and rhythms. Where we get tripped up is when we see another's progression, whether stranger or friend, as opposition to our own.

When our eyes are on others and what they have, they're not on God and what He offers. So how do we stop comparing our seasons to others'? While the Bible doesn't feature any books written in dating-show style, that doesn't mean it's void of wisdom in every season and situation, including comparison in singleness.

In Mark 5 we meet Jairus, a man who can teach us about comparison. Upon Jesus' arrival in Capernaum, Jairus, one of the synagogue leaders, met Him and hit his knees, pleading with Christ to come quickly to heal his dying daughter. Moved, Jesus agreed and started walking with him to his home. I can easily picture the internal sigh of relief

Jairus breathed as he started back in the direction of where his pains and answers rested, in tandem with the One who could revive them.

But then the crowd started to creep in. If I were in Jairus's shoes, I'd become that holiday shopper again, with my shoulders tensing the closer others came. "Stay back from my Jesus. He's working on *my* behalf right now."

While they were walking, Jesus sensed someone touch Him and stopped in His tracks to address the crowd. His disciples confusedly assured Him that many people likely had touched Him, as they were amid a large group. All the while I'm sure Jairus thought, *Thanks for keeping Him on track, guys, now let's get going again.* But Jesus didn't continue walking. He "kept looking around to see who had [touched him]. Then the woman, knowing what had happened to her, came and fell at his feet and, trembling with fear, told him the whole truth. He said to her, 'Daughter, your faith has healed you. Go in peace and be freed from your suffering'" (Mark 5:32–34 NIV).

This woman in the crowd had suffered an internal bleeding issue for twelve years, and upon seeing Jesus decided if she could just touch Him she would be healed. Our Healer saw this faith worth pausing to address—a welcomed interruption. However, I'm sure Jairus wasn't so thrilled about stopping on the journey of bringing healing to his heart's great concern. Especially as the story continues, "While Jesus was still speaking, some people came from the house of Jairus, the synagogue leader. 'Your daughter is dead,' they said. 'Why bother the teacher anymore?'" (v. 35 NIV).

I do not believe our comparative actions always stem from jealousy and envy so much as doubt and fear. When we see the Lord's healings and giftings coming to fruition in others' lives, while we feel we've been passed over, what do we do? How do we keep faith when our doubts are saying, *You've been waiting for X number of years. You think it's still worth it? Why do you even bother anymore?*

Mark's gospel says Jairus was earnest and positioned himself to encounter Jesus with faith (5:22–23 NIV), yet his petition was still delayed behind another's. The error here would be to lose trust in Jesus. Instead, even in delay we should be like Jairus and obey Jesus, who said, "Don't be afraid; just believe" (v. 36 NIV). While we're walking with God, we can wonder, *Why is He moving so slowly? He seems to be touching everyone else but me, and I asked first!* But do not forget the power of the mere fact that Christ is walking with you!

We must keep truth and hope close in our hearts to combat the lies of comparison before they arise. Mimic David and tell your fears to flee and your heart to rise in strength (Ps. 27:1). Someone else beginning a relationship does not steal a chance from you, because yours is not up for grabs. When the naysayers or doubters say there's no way, trust there is always a way for goodness and grace when God is in the story.

Jairus had to throw off impatience and hopelessness and keep trusting Jesus:

> When they came to the home of the synagogue leader, Jesus saw a commotion, with people crying and wailing loudly. He went in and said to them, "Why all this commotion and wailing? The child is not dead but asleep." But they laughed at him . . .
>
> [Jesus] took the child's father and mother and the disciples who were with him, and went in where the child was. He took her by the hand and said to her, "*Talitha koum!*" (which means "Little girl, I say to you, get up!"). Immediately the girl stood up and began to walk around. . . . At this they were completely astonished. (Mark 5:38–42 NIV)

The Lord is a true triple threat: omnipotent, omniscient, and omnipresent. He's omnipotent in that His power is unlimited and does not diminish. We need not fear that in doing for others, He will have less for us. He's omniscient in that His wisdom stretches behind and before all things. He knows if, when, and whom you will marry. He won't accidentally appoint your destined spouse to someone else. And He is omnipresent, as He is everywhere; He is outside of time. His "yes" to someone else does not have to translate to a "no" for you—He can work on your behalf and others' simultaneously.

While Jesus' human form was encountering Jairus and the bleeding woman one at a time, His heavenly attributes were at work behind the scenes. Not once were these individuals or miracles in competition or opposition. If we don't want to limit God in what He can do for us, then we cannot limit Him in what He can do for others. If our desires rested in only our own ability to make things come to pass, the comparison, envy, jealousy, and fear would make sense. But we do not serve a God who leaves us to fend for ourselves or leads us to have to strive against others for His blessings.

A heart at peace gives life to the body,
but envy rots the bones. (Prov. 14:30 NIV)

COMPETITORS TO COMPANIONS

What's truly wonderful is when we find those we once saw as competitors become companions. Personally, I've seen relationships between women who seemed to always be laced with rivalry soften into true admiration for one another. But this transformation is not effortless. It will require you to alter your inclinations and instigate change.

Think of a friendship or relationship you want to better—either someone you've drifted away from or a person you're in proximity with, but there's an underlying tension between you two you can't put your finger on. If you're inclined to turn away from this person because of what they have, turn to them with what you have on your mind. If you feel there's a juxtaposition of tension, put yourself in a position of listening and seeking to make them feel safe. If things often come to a head between you both, lower yourself before them in humility.

Not only will this effort on your part help dispel comparison from your mind, but it will also cultivate a powerful muscle in you. Successful relationships, platonic and romantic, require us to be people who are slow to anger and quick to listen (James 1:19). Your gentleness and caring heart will serve you far better than doubt and comparison.

In the intermixing of community there are the categories of *yours*, *mine*, and *ours*. There will be things others have that you don't: dreams, abilities, talents, or paths. That's okay; those are for them. And vice versa, there will be things you cherish or fight for that cannot be taken from you—they are yours. And still other things will merge in your stories. When we know what is ours, celebrate others in what is theirs, and share the joy in what is ours together, we thwart the Enemy's plan for division and comparison not only in our love lives but in the fullness of life itself.

So as you pray for your future husband and wait on Jesus to fulfill your deepest desires or bring comfort in times of pain, remember this: He's always walking with you, working in ways you may not yet see. Sometimes He will bring blessings and answers in someone else's story before revealing His plan for yours. He hasn't departed or forgotten your route. Rather than becoming rivals, we are called to be co-benefactors—cheering each other on as we watch God do immeasurably more than we could ever imagine, plan, or prepare for on our own (Eph. 3:20).

> SOMETIMES HE WILL BRING BLESSINGS AND ANSWERS IN SOMEONE ELSE'S STORY BEFORE REVEALING HIS PLAN FOR YOURS.

When we pray for others—whether friends, sisters, or even those we're tempted to compare ourselves to—we open our hearts to God's greater plan and experience His goodness in more ways than we see only in our own story. Praying for others not only expands our perspective but also cultivates grace, joy, and trust in His perfect timing. In blessing others, we often find our journeys enriched in ways we never expected. So keep praying boldly, for yourself and for those around you, because love and faith grow strongest when they're shared.

CHAPTER 9

BECAUSE WHY NOT?

You may be wondering, *What if I pray and nothing changes? Does praying for your future husband really work?* Well, that depends on what you define as "work." Is the change you're hoping to see something quick in your status or an inner working within you now, that develops outwardly later? Look, I know that by praying for our future husbands, we're hoping it comes with a last-name change . . . and sooner rather than later. But there is more that God wants to do within us and through our time in prayer than altering our initials.

The truth is, going through this book cannot quicken or guarantee your husband's arrival date. I wish I could promise two-day shipping for a date with your husband like Amazon Prime. Alas, I cannot. God is the boss in the delivery process, and for good reason. Because the faith produced in adhering to His authority is far greater than a delivery guarantee. He's not a genie in a bottle; He is our heavenly Father who brings things forward in perfect timing rather than by instant request.

Though I vividly remember wishing sometimes it were the other way around, I promise this way is better!

There is the chance that you could be waiting awhile until you meet your spouse, or that being married could not be God's purpose for you. So why even pray if a husband is not guaranteed? Well, think about it: When do you ever pray with guarantees or control? Why would we even pray if control or guarantees were ours?

Think back to the last time you went for a job interview. Chances are, you did not have control over what questions the interviewer would ask, nor a guarantee that you'd get the position. Did that stop you from showing up as your best, answering the questions authentically, and believing you could see yourself at this company? Surely not. If it did, wouldn't that have hurt your likelihood of receiving the outcome you desired?

Praying for your future spouse isn't a maneuver to hurry the process; rather, it is a way to cover your partner in prayer and heighten your vision for what is to come.

I believe part of the hesitancy we have in asking God for answers or miracles is from thinking we'll be let down if we don't receive what we ask, or we will be a letdown to God if we ask for the wrong thing.

Jesus Himself dealt with both these ideas simultaneously. We get a glimpse into this mental battle through His prayer on the Mount of Olives: "Father, if you are willing, remove this cup from me. Nevertheless, not my will, but yours, be done" (Luke 22:42).

PRAYING FOR YOUR FUTURE SPOUSE ISN'T A MANEUVER TO HURRY THE PROCESS; RATHER, IT IS A WAY TO COVER YOUR PARTNER IN PRAYER AND HEIGHTEN YOUR VISION FOR WHAT IS TO COME.

If Jesus could bring His desires and requests to God the Father—asking freely and trusting fully in the outcome—then I'd say you and I can follow His model.

If doubt or uncertainty creeps in, our thoughts can drift: *Perhaps it'd be better if I wait until I meet the guy I think I'll marry before I start praying, because I don't want to be let down or do this wrong.* Let's continue reading Luke 22. After Jesus made His petition to the Father, He left His place of prayer to find the disciples sleeping from their sorrow. Christ ridiculed them for sleeping at such a time (vv. 45–46). I want to ask you, Why would we take the position of sleeping when we could take the position of prayer?

As someone who wrestles with control, I get it. But better than control is surrender, and better than guarantee is hope.

No, you don't know for certain if and when your true love will appear. But what if he does? How will you want to look back on the ways you prepared for your marriage, nurtured your desire for love, and blessed his arrival? Why pray for your future husband? I think the better question is, Why *not* pray for the man you're believing for?

A HUSBAND IS NOT A PRIZE

As I've emphasized throughout this book, it is important that you turn to Scripture as you walk this path of singleness. So let's look there to see the will of God regarding marriage.

- "It is God's will that you should be sanctified" (1 Thess. 4:3 NIV).
- "Give thanks in all circumstances; for this is the will of God in Christ Jesus for you" (1 Thess. 5:18).
- "For this is the will of God, that by doing good you should put to silence the ignorance of foolish people" (1 Peter 2:15).
- "He has told you, O man, what is good; and what does the LORD require of you but to do justice, and to love kindness, and to walk humbly with your God?" (Mic. 6:8).

God's will is for us to be set apart, grateful, wise, and to walk righteously. He wants you to live in this manner, and perhaps if He sees marriage as an enhancer to those, then you'll walk in them with a spouse. If God has it for you and you are walking with Him earnestly, He will make a way for it to come to you.

Celebrating seven years of marriage this year, I can attest that God has brought forth purposeful refinement, enhancement, and goodness through my relationship. But marriage was a vehicle through which He brought forth His purpose for me. Oftentimes the idea creeps in that our life begins after we say "I do," or that our purpose is in either being a wife or mother or an established, successful woman. But His purpose already dwells richly within you, just as you are right now and as you develop. Wherever we are, in whatever season of life or relationship status, God's will always prevails.

If or when you marry, your husband should not be considered a prize. I wrote in my previous book, *Break Up with What Broke You*, that a husband is a treasure we cherish and steward. Gifts are freely given while prizes are won or earned. The Lord gives His people good gifts—gifts of wisdom, faith, mercy, healing, leadership, and so on. These gifts God gives are not possessions to show off or prizes to place on a shelf. A husband is not a reward for good behavior or good faith, reserved only for the lucky few. Marriage is not an act of luck, superiority, or gain—it is a commitment. Every good and perfect gift the Lord bestows is an entrustment that is meant to better us for our service and for those we serve (our relationships, our purpose, and our devotion).

While marriage is not a reward, it does require of us righteousness to carry it well. We pray for our future husbands because we want to be good stewards of the men we are believing for. When praying for a coming marriage, God is our goal and a husband a potential gift.

Your marriage is a bestowal and a vessel—something to honor and keep, an avenue for giving and receiving love, and supplying accountability. There is palpable power in praying for your future husband, even in your current state or season. Before you know his name or before you're even ready to date, prayer offers protection, preparation, and provision. Plainly speaking, it keeps your eyes set on the *true* prize—the heart posture and ability to glorify God in any and everything we do.

GRAVEYARD SHIFTS AND GOD'S SURPRISES

Do you know any night owls? You know, the ones who work late hours and early mornings while the rest of us are snuggled up in bed? I'm talking about the medics, firefighters, and red-eye pilots. These personnel work what's called the graveyard shift, usually staying awake all through the night, sundown to sunup. I don't know how they do it!

Much of what they do goes unseen. But though their work can go undetected or unnoticed, it does not diminish it. A doctor can save a life, a firefighter can stop a catastrophe, and a pilot can safely deliver one hundred people to their destination, all with hardly anyone to notice. While the world is asleep, they are at work.

God's surprises can be found in the graveyard shift.

"I foretold the former things long ago, my mouth announced them and I made them known; then suddenly I acted, and they came to pass." (Isa. 48:3 NIV)

While we're unaware, He is toiling on our behalf, working things out and weaving them together. In the night, in the delay, in the waiting, we may not see what is occurring, but I promise you He is up to more than we can sense.

I knew a lot of Emilys, Hannahs, and Madisons growing up, but I find it ironic that three of the most mentioned women in Jesus' ministry all shared the same name: *Mary*. Mary Magdalene, Mary the mother of

Jesus, and Mary the mother of James and Joseph. *Mary, did you know your name would be so favored?*

Imagine how scenarios unfolded when two or three of them were all together! Such as the moment on the cross; or when the women went to anoint Jesus' body but it was gone. They were stunned! I can almost picture the scene as they rushed back to the disciples and explained what happened: "Okay, so Mary went in first and gasped . . . Then Mary followed and shrieked . . . Then Mary said, 'Wait—what's going on?'"

At that point, Peter was probably saying, "Hold on, *which* Mary are we even talking about?"

But the common name is not what's most baffling in this story; it's the fact that the status of a leader and the fate of an entire people group were changed overnight. While eyes were shut tight, dreaming unaware, something unfathomable occurred. During the graveyard shift, the grave was conquered!

Though I cannot promise you that leaning into your desire and meeting it with faith and dedication grants a quick relationship change, it does yield a return. When we ask God to do a work in us now for what He has prepared later, He will! Once we seek to honor God in our being and in our relationship, we see the fruit of it.

God knows where, who, and when is best for you to be married according to His will, *and* He has so much in store for you ahead of and after the wedding day you dream of. I trust the wisdom of Matthew 7:7, "Ask, and it will be given to you; seek, and you will find; knock, and it will be opened to you."

These prayers will sharpen you in who you're becoming, benefit you and your future spouse, and keep you off the wrong paths. To me, that is a trifold "yes, this works." It works so much greater and in so many more ways than a quick delivery; it creates within us a resounding assurance of God's protection and preparation. Prayer is powerful—this we know to be true.

As we close this section, I want you to meditate on the following thoughts and questions:

- *Imagine the kind of marriage and partnership you desire. What qualities in a future spouse are you most prayerful for, that you would be most grateful for?*
- *What dreams or goals do you hope to share with your future spouse?*
- *Write a prayer of gratitude, thanking God for preparing both you and your future spouse according to His perfect plan.*
- *Reflect on a time when God answered a prayer in a way that was better than you imagined. How does this encourage you to trust Him now?*
- *Think of a situation where waiting resulted in a greater blessing than you anticipated. How does that inspire your gratitude today?*
- *What scriptures bring you comfort and hope as you wait for God's timing? Write them down and thank God for His promises.*
- *What qualities or skills are you developing that will bless your future marriage?*

PART 2

HOW TO *Pray*

Introduction

HOW DO I PRAY WITHOUT BECOMING OBSESSED?

When you're hoping, believing, and praying for a heart desire, where's the line in expectation versus obsession?

In full transparency, when it came to praying for my future husband, I had a mix of hope and hesitation. On one hand, I *wanted* to believe God cared about this deep desire of mine. But on the other, I didn't want to become so focused on marriage that I lost myself—or worse, lost sight of God. If you're anything like me, you've probably asked, *Am I doing this right? Can I pray for my future husband without getting swept up in the idea of him?*

I believe the answer is yes—but with some heart checks along the way.

Early on, I realized two things:

1. I desperately needed God's guidance in dating because, left to my own devices, I made a mess of things.
2. God didn't want me to only pray for a husband but to spend time with Him—keeping Him my *first* love before asking Him for my *coming* love.

Now, I'm the kind of person who can turn anything into a passion project. When I do something, I go all in, sometimes allowing what I feel in a moment to trump what I need in the long term. Praying for my future husband had to be intentional. So I made a practice: Before I opened the Bible I had bought for my future husband, I opened mine. I'd meet with God myself first—because if I wasn't grounded in Him, I risked giving someone else the space that only God is meant to hold.

Many of the women I've connected with have understood this and shared the sentiment, maybe even more than was necessary. Some women have told me they've stopped praying for a husband out of fear of idolization—hearing advice such as "Be careful, you don't want to make your husband an idol." Let's be real though. No one says that when we pray for a job, a home, healing, or even friendships. The solution isn't silence; it's alignment. When you keep God at the center, your prayers for your future spouse can actually *draw you closer* to Him. Because faith is the assurance of things unseen (Heb. 11:1)—the practice of asking, believing, and trusting in God for His plan.

So the *act* of praying for your future husband isn't the problem. The problem is when that desire becomes *bigger* than your desire for God.

How do you know if your desire for your future husband has become an idol? Consider these questions:

- Are you talking *to* God, or just talking *at* Him about your spouse?
- Have you started believing marriage will fix the problem areas in your life?
- Is this the only area where you're exercising faith?

If the answer is yes—or even maybe a teeny, tiny bit yes—to any of these questions, that's all right. Stay with me. We don't have to throw that desire away, but let's recenter.

If we want a marriage that's truly lasting and deeply fulfilling, it must be built on something stronger than emotion or desire; it must be centered on Christ. So often in our longing to be loved, we unintentionally place the weight of our hope on the hope for a husband—believing once we're married, we'll finally feel complete, secure, or whole. But that expectation turns our future spouse into something they were never meant to be: a savior.

No matter how godly, loving, or supportive he is, your future husband cannot take the role or responsibilities of Jesus—He is the only One who can meet your deepest needs, redeem your story, and bring lasting peace.

I love marriage. I wouldn't write an entire book on it if I didn't. But marriage is a beautiful gift, not the promised land. Once you understand that your husband is an addition to the good work Christ has already begun in you—not the entirety—you can find more joy in every season and thrive in your marriage. Your relationship, when it comes, will be a blessing, not a rescue. When both of your hearts are anchored in Christ, your future marriage becomes a space where His presence can richly dwell, where love is not simply felt but is rooted in something eternal.

So as you wait and pray, remember this: Intimacy with God is the foundation for our lives, and our marriages.

Let your heart rest in the truth that you are already fully known, fully loved, and fully seen by the One who will never leave you. And as you grow closer to Him, you'll be prepared not only for marriage but for a life that reflects His glory in every season.

Even if your prayers start out messy, repetitive, or timid, that's okay—keep showing up. David often began his prayers grumpy or greedy, but by the end became grounded. How? Because just as time in prayer can change our circumstances, it can also do more than that—it can change *us*.

> BECAUSE JUST AS TIME IN PRAYER CAN CHANGE OUR CIRCUMSTANCES, IT CAN ALSO DO MORE THAN THAT—IT CAN CHANGE *US*.

In the chapters ahead, I want to show you *how* to pray for your future husband. We'll introduce six mindful and applicable practices you can implement during your time in prayer to move in faith without hesitancy or obsession, but expectation and hope.

CHAPTER 10

PRAY WITH HEAVENLY WISDOM

Seconds after stepping through the door, the scent greets you—notes of herbs and seasoning burst in front of you like decadent fireworks. Your tastebuds begin dancing on your tongue as you breathe in the familiar, delicious scent of your grandmother's coveted dish. This is her masterpiece—the specialty plate she makes every Thanksgiving or Christmas. Relatives may even fight over who gets to inherit Mamaw's recipe.

There's an entire literary market dedicated to cookbooks because people will pay good money to know the secrets of kitchen successes. A warm and delicious meal can nourish the body's needs and nurture a gathering of people. Cookbooks help bring ingredients to life through detailed instruction. They tell us how much of a certain ingredient to add. Or explain when to add baking soda or baking powder, and thankfully someone knows the difference between the two because I sure don't. An informative recipe can help even the most novice chefs and bakers feel confident enough to try their hand in the kitchen.

In the same way you're more likely to make a delicious dish rather than a tasteless mush if you follow a recipe, in relationships you're more likely to have a positive result if you follow wisdom. So how do you find it? Maybe you dream of having a love like your parents', or maybe you have never seen a healthy, godly marriage up close yet still desire to live one yourself. What's the recipe for a great, lasting marriage? Well, the recipe can vary based on your flavor preferences, but I'll tell you the *one* ingredient that is vital in every marriage recipe—prayer.

Whether your idea of the perfect cake is classic red velvet or decadent rich chocolate, one thing stays the same: What's inside determines how it turns out. And just like you wouldn't expect a cake to rise without the right ingredients, you can't expect a Christ-centered marriage to thrive without passionate prayer, radical faith, and the wisdom of the Holy Spirit.

You may have gravitated to this book because praying for your future husband seems daunting. Where do you start? How long or how often? When I started praying for my future husband, I sought organization but wanted to leave room for spontaneous prompting. I firmly believe that prayer is fluid and authentic, an all-applicable, widely beneficial tool for our lives.

The purpose of prayer is to show our faith in God, surrendering every part of our hearts and every possible path to Him. Prayer is supplication, dedication, communication, and regulation. Christ Himself prayed to the Father to direct Him and discipline His inner workings to align with God's perfect will.

PRAYER IS SUPPLICATION, DEDICATION, COMMUNICATION, AND REGULATION.

Prayer will strengthen our affections and directions to coordinate with God, enabling us to lean less on ourselves and our own ways (Isa. 55:9) and increase our trust in His perfect plans. Prayer also guards our hearts, like bumpers at a bowling alley, keeping us from going into the gutter by reminding us our objective is to worship Him (Dan. 2:20). Our objective as His daughters is to glorify Him in all we do—including in our marriages.

Every time we pray, we are touching the hem of His garment—positioning ourselves in reliance on Him and in proximity to His power. No matter where you've come from, what kind of love you have witnessed or wanted, every single one of us can utilize and benefit from powerful, faithful, Holy Spirit–led prayer. It is the crucial ingredient in our recipe for a love that overcomes obstacles, rises to challenges, and lasts through the seasons.

A few women have shared with me how it's hard to stay consistent in prayer. Others say they don't know exactly what to pray for:

- "How do I know what attributes to cover? How do I know everything he needs covering for?"
- "What if I miss something?"
- "I ran out of ideas after the first time . . . What do I do?"

It's incredibly common to begin praying and find yourself at a loss for what to pray or get distracted and lose your train of thought. Sometimes a visual reminder, prayer outline, or focused topic can help spur our passions or steady our overstimulated minds to better enter into our time of prayer. My hope is this book will help you accomplish this!

So if you've felt a little confused about how to pray for your future husband, you're not alone. Even the disciples benefited from instruction for their prayers. In Matthew 6 Jesus gave them an example for how to pray (vv. 9–13). What does this teach us about praying for our desire for marriage? I believe it imparts to us that prayer must be authentic and sincere. It also shows God wants to meet us and direct us as we pray so that our time with Him is effective.

God doesn't only hear our prayers; He guides them too.

The next time you get ready to pray, use the following three practices to help you welcome heavenly wisdom into your prayer time.

PRAY PASSIONATELY

Prayer must be passionate, or else why pray at all? Romans 12:11 says, "Never be lacking in zeal, but keep your spiritual fervor, serving the Lord" (NIV).

Passion doesn't translate to a set volume, timeline, or number of Scripture references. Passion is measured inwardly. You may be an extroverted, top-of-your-lungs shouter, or maybe you're a reserved, crisscross-applesauce-seated, soft-and-sweet type. Whichever style is truer to your personality, let passion drench your words and drip from your heart.

I love that there are two definitions for *passion* by Oxford Languages. The first definition is "strong and barely controllable emotion." The second is "the suffering and death of Jesus."[1] Christ modeled passion in His love for us and His giving of Himself. This action was undeniably bold, heartfelt, and moving. His body was bloody and bruised, while His countenance was poised and reticent. Passion is embodied through our inner thoughts and outer actions, private emotions and shared expressions alike. Passion can be expressed in different ways at different times, but it must remain alive and active.

Pray passionately in the Spirit, as you constantly intercede with every form of prayer at all times. (Eph. 6:17–18 TPT)

Some days it's easier to scroll, sigh, or settle than it is to pray boldly. But passionate prayer shifts things—starting with our own hearts.

It's not about being dramatic; it's about being honest and expectant, trusting God hears and responds when we lean in with everything we've got.

We don't need halfhearted, half-doubting prayers but rather prayers that are just scary enough to make us rely on God's faithfulness to move mountains. We get the chance to pray for more than we can see or imagine—how incredible!

PRAY WITH FAITH

While most people would love to be in love, for some, the idea of falling out of love is scary. I understand why that concern exists. With a disheartening 40 to 50 percent divorce rate in the United States,[2] it's no wonder some are scared to take the plunge. *What if it doesn't work out?*

Here's a reassuring statistic: Seventy-four percent of marriages where the couple attends church together last. Not bad, but wait, there's more! There's an even better secret weapon available. Statistics show that only 1 in 1,500 marriages where the couple prays together end in divorce.[3] That is a 99.93 percent success rate! How amazing that (1) I could properly do that math, and (2) prayer makes such a difference! I wish I had a success stat for the couples where individuals prayed *for* each other before getting married; maybe one day.

Results like this show that faith is powerful and profitable.

In Exodus chapters 3 and 4, when God spoke to Moses through the burning bush, He needed Moses to be full of faith before He fulfilled anything through him. All the mighty deeds God would work through Moses first relied on him having faith. Faith that God was who He said He was and He would go before him. Moses also had to have faith God knew what He was doing. Having lived in the desert for decades, he was now an outsider without familiarity or influence. I'm sure Moses would have preferred that God quietly deliver the people to him and snuck them out, rather than confront Pharaoh—or that He provide a special camel escort instead of having them run from the Egyptian army.

When we ask God to move or He tells us to move in a direction, focusing on the outcome will keep us stagnant or skittish. Imagine a kid on a road trip pestering their parents by constantly asking, "Are we there yet?" In our juvenile understanding of all God's mighty works, we're like children who know we are on a journey but cannot comprehend how long it takes or which direction is best. We have to trust the one driving the car. A child wouldn't know you should take a few backroads because interstate I-65 has a hazard, or that you need to stop when you're low on gas or hungry because there are not many stations available farther ahead on the journey.

We may not understand why God's timeline seems slow or why we have to take certain steps in our walk, but when we pray with faith, we remain moving in the right direction, even when our earthly eyes cannot yet tell why it was the right path.

Prayer without faith is futile. It's possible to get caught in the motions of prayer and the habit of being a Christian, so the Word warns us not to let our faith grow dormant, even while our lips are still praying. Isaiah 29:13 cautions, "The Lord says: 'These people come near to me with their mouth and honor me with their lips, but their hearts are far from me. Their worship of me is based on merely human rules they have been taught'" (NIV).

Faith is expectant, not contingent.

Keep your faith alive! Like a fire ablaze, let it shine in front of others and kindle a closeness with the Lord. When we draw near in faith, we are met by His presence—the best answer to prayer we can ever receive. His Spirit moves on our behalf, speaks to us through our requests, and comforts us in our situations. When we are moved by faith, we are relying on the Holy Spirit.

FAITH IS EXPECTANT, NOT CONTINGENT.

PRAY WITH THE HOLY SPIRIT

I'd be remiss to share about praying for your husband without highlighting the power and necessity of depending on the Holy Spirit.

Did you ever have a new kid join your school after the school year had begun? All the other students were already acquainted and had formed their groups and cliques with their shared interests, sports, or clubs. When this new arrival came halfway through the semester, it was easy for the whole school to catch a story of who they were and what they were like through the rumor mill before anyone had a chance to speak to them.

In many ways, that's how we can treat the Holy Spirit. We may be familiar with the Lord God and Jesus Christ, but the Holy Spirit can feel like the "new kid" in our spiritual understanding. We've heard about Him briefly in church (hopefully), maybe even formed opinions, but have we taken the time to truly get to know Him? The truth is, He's not new at all—He's been present from the beginning—leading, comforting, and empowering us. The more we welcome Him, the more clearly we hear God's voice and walk in His wisdom.

Your familiarity with this expression of God's divinity can vary based on how you were introduced to Him. Maybe growing up, the term "Holy Ghost" felt a little too mystical or His Spirit was rarely mentioned in Sunday services. Either way, your starting point shapes how comfortable—or cautious—you might feel about embracing the Holy Spirit today. But know this: The Holy Spirit is not weird or eerie! Nor is He complicated or overpowering.

Put simply, we know God is a supreme being who expresses Himself in three forms: God the Father, Jesus Christ the Son, and Holy Spirit the Advocate and Helper. The Holy Spirit is God's wisdom and comfort sent to guide us through our days. When Jesus told His disciples about His impending departure, He reminded them not to be dismayed because it was *good* for them to receive the Spirit: "Nevertheless, I tell you the truth: it is to your advantage that I go away, for if I do not go away, the Helper will not come to you. But if I go, I will send him to you" (John 16:7). I can just imagine Peter saying, "This new guy over *You*, Jesus? What are You thinking?"

Jesus knew that He would pave the way for us to enter heaven, and next up was the Holy Spirit. He wasn't a replacement or lesser version; He was and is exactly what we need to live in power, faith, and righteousness. He is our Helper—enabling us to live a faithful life in all things, including dating and marriage. The Holy Spirit speaks to us through wisdom, conviction, peace, and prophecy. Let's look at how these areas are beneficial in praying for our spouse and marriage.

- **Wisdom**: Wisdom from the Spirit instructs us how to be godly in all areas. It's the kind of insight that empowers us to speak life when someone has hurt us, be patient when our day is overrun, and love when we've been offended. We're not required to know all the answers for ourselves, but to rely on the One who does.
- **Conviction**: In dating especially, it's important to adhere to conviction the Spirit gives. If we are moving too fast with someone or lines are getting blurred, conviction reels us back for our minds and bodies to remain in step with righteousness.
- **Peace**: The peace of God comforts us when ease seems impossible and steadies us when eagerness can catch us off guard. The peace that comes from the Spirit is like our anchor, keeping us steady when the waves around us are dangerously stormy or excitingly rising.
- **Prophecy**: This spiritual insight isn't only for prediction; prophecy is for protection, encouragement, aid, and sharing God's heart. In relationships this can allow us to pray for or even speak up on specific insights for our partner.

The Spirit will direct us. Don't let the *hows* get in the way of the hope!

Whenever we feel conflicted or confused, even when we don't know what to pray, the Spirit is there to lead us in comfort and clarity. Romans 8:26 says that when we pray, the Spirit intercedes for us according to the Father's will. Now, that doesn't sound eerie to me; it sounds like the best wingman we could possibly have! Because, honestly, who hasn't been on a date and thought, *Jesus, take the wheel!*

While heavenly wisdom is probably the last thing we're thinking of as a solution to relationship confusion or questions—because it's habit to go to YouTube for dating advice or to a friend to decode what your date's text *really* meant—it is the first thing we should seek. We benefit greatly from the Holy Spirit's guidance in singleness, discernment during dating, and empowerment throughout marriage.

If the Lord wants to speak to you through His Messenger, make sure the lines of communication are open.

When we pray with bold faith and lean into the power of the Holy Spirit, something beautiful happens: God begins to align our hearts with His and we readily sense His direction. Walking in step with the Holy Spirit—depending on Him, listening to His promptings, and honoring Him in our choices—shapes how we live, love, and make decisions.

Ephesians 4:30 tells us that we've been *sealed* by the Holy Spirit. So let your heart rest in that promise. And from that place, lean on His wisdom to guide your next steps—whether it's in prayer, dating, healing, or learning to trust again.

CHAPTER 11

PRAY WITH EXPECTATION

As the sun glistened off the river, my dad stood beside me like a proud coach, rattling off instructions. "Bait, line, and hook." I nodded like I understood, but truthfully, I was more focused on not dropping my cute pink Barbie pole into the water.

I can still picture my tiny self, standing there with sun-kissed cheeks, pigtails bouncing, and a life jacket so snug it nearly swallowed me whole as my dad taught me how to fish—or at least he *tried* to.

There was a lot to remember! I had been under the impression you just tossed the bobber in and waited for the fish to take the bait. Well, it turns out, fishing is harder than it looks. It requires patience, skill, and a kind of precision that eight-year-old me definitely didn't have. You can't just show up, fling your line, and expect to snag a giant bass worthy of a guy's dating profile picture—grinning ear to ear, fish stretched out like a trophy.

But what did I know as a novice fisher with a pink plastic pole? Let's look from Peter's perspective, a professional fisherman who knew the art of fishing well. He spent years on the water, often experiencing his own long hours of waiting with limited success. But one morning after he had been fishing all night with zero luck, he was about ready to give up, when along came this hippie-like stranger yelling from the shore, "Hey, man, throw in the net again!" (Luke 5:4, my paraphrase). Peter humored him and suddenly fish started swarming into the net like there was a BOGO sale going on (v. 6). You know Peter had to be thinking, *What just happened? Who is this guy?*

He likely wasn't expecting to get shown up in his craft by some dude in sandals giving unsolicited fishing advice. But that's exactly how Jesus operates—outside of our expectations. And that was just the beginning! He had a habit of showing up in ways no one anticipated, especially not the people closest to Him.

Just imagine how flabbergasted the disciples must have constantly been around Jesus! As soon as they started to understand how He operated and what He was capable of, *boom!*—another "who is this guy?!" moment. He consistently challenged their assumptions and bypassed their expectations.

- They didn't expect Jesus to turn five loaves of bread and two fish into a heavenly buffet for over five thousand people (Matt. 14:13–21).
- They didn't expect Jesus to so freely welcome lepers, sinners, and little children with open arms (Luke 5:12–16, 29–32; 18:16).
- They didn't expect Him, the One to be served, to willingly serve them by washing their feet (John 13:1–15).
- They didn't expect Jesus to conquer the Enemy by dying on a cross and claiming victory through resurrection (Matt. 28:1–10).

Yet, He did all this—and more!

Honestly, we can't blame the disciples for being thrown off. Most of them were teenagers, following the most radical, wise, and wildly unpredictable man ever to walk the earth. Surprise was kinda part of the deal. Because Jesus didn't come to meet our expectations—He came to *exceed* them.

Now to him who is able to do far more abundantly than all that we ask or think, according to the power at work within us, to him be glory in the church and in Christ Jesus throughout all generations, forever and ever. Amen. (Eph. 3:20–21)

The Lord, in all His splendor and majesty, will surely surprise us too. His very nature and goodness are higher than we can comprehend. He simply doesn't fit inside the limits of our minds. Even if we can't predict exactly what He will do, I want you to expect that He will move!

> JESUS DIDN'T COME TO MEET OUR EXPECTATIONS—HE CAME TO *EXCEED* THEM.

You may not have seen yet how His plan will unfold for your desire for a marriage, but what *have* you witnessed of His goodness? Perhaps you've experienced God:

- heal you or a loved one of a disease or diagnosis,
- comfort someone's heart and bring them to faith, or
- comfort you with peace and love in a time you felt utterly heartbroken.

All the testimonies of God, from the Word or our lives, prove that He is wonderful and works in mighty, mysterious ways. Let your appreciation of who He is and what He has already done fuel your expectation of what He is still doing and will do.

Do you believe that God is good and has good things in store for you? Maybe you *did* but after delay or disappointment you've started to wonder. Not everyone will be able to empathize with that feeling, but I know someone who can and whose story is full of understanding and triumph.

Recently on my podcast I interviewed my friend Mia Fieldes Dunnavant, a songwriter known for cowriting worship anthems such as "Yes I Will" and "Peace Be Still"—anthems of trusting in the waiting that she formed from her own life lessons.[1] She'd seen God move in her life in radical ways, like overcoming poverty and believing at thirteen to write powerful worship ballads that would be heard all over the world. But in dating she was left waiting—waiting through her teens, twenties, and thirties for the promise of marriage to be fulfilled. One day God told her He wanted to heal something within her—disappointment. How many of us would be brave enough to admit we've carried some of that in the waiting?

She felt the Lord tell her, *I have something custom-made for you, but custom-made things take a little longer.*[2] Though not without its challenges and misunderstandings by well-meaning others, she journeyed in faith and hope. And a few years later, when she met Joren, her now-husband, it was clear: God had been writing a beautiful story all along.

Maybe you're at a place where you're saying, "I'm ready to let go—of disappointment, of control, of fear—and trust God with fresh expectation." Whether it's for the first time or the first time in a while, that's a powerful turning point.

But what does it actually look like to live with expectation? And what does it require of you *right now*?

Expectation is preparation. It's not passive hope; it's active faith. One of the most powerful ways to fuel that expectation is through consistent, intentional prayer. Prayer keeps your heart expectant in

God's goodness and promises, even when your circumstances haven't changed—*yet.*

EXPECT TO BE ACTIVE

Do you ever feel you're twiddling your thumbs through singleness? *Yes, but what else am I supposed to do . . . I'm just waiting!*

There are two types of waiting, and they produce different results: *reactive* waiting and *active* waiting. One makes us subject to all the things we can't control—like the hands on a clock. The other makes us present to all we can derive from the time. Within dating, or more precisely singleness, these approaches can alter how we process and progress.

Let's break them down.

Reactive waiting means you're responding or echoing rather than initiating. You're reacting to other events that are occurring around you while you're "on pause," or echoing the questions playing in your mind or that others have asked you. "Why are you still single? You're such a catch!" *Hmm . . . why* am *I still single?* This type of waiting makes way for emotions to arise. Those emotions can be bitterness from the time spent waiting or jealousy from desiring someone else's story.

Conversely, active waiting means you have a plan in place. *Um, Christian, my plan was to be married by twenty-three!* No, not that kind of fixed-timeline plan. I mean a plan for each season. We are not the masters of our grand schedule, but we do determine what we gain from where God has us.

Remaining active means remaining in Christ—trusting that at the right time, with the right person, in the right way, God will swiftly bring forth His plans to completion (Isa. 60:22). That means no forcing, no rushing, just trusting—easier said than done, I know. But that's part of the beauty in this!

Praying is active waiting.

When it's winter, we crave the warm sunshine and ocean air, then in summer we miss watching snowflakes fall while sipping peppermint hot chocolate. It's natural to dream of what the next season will bring, but we shouldn't miss out on the season we're in by yearning for a season we've not yet entered.

Being active in prayerful, expectant hope and intentional singleness offers activities unique to this season. There is so much at our disposal while we are single that isn't always available in later seasons. It's a time for unhurried reflection and exploration, rich development and discovery, and creative expression. As a single woman who's active and present in her singleness, you have time and space to pursue your interests, socialize, and give back. Host a weekly dinner or Bible study with friends, enroll in an extracurricular class or take up rock climbing, volunteer in your community or church, learn how to bake sourdough or make pottery, do any and everything that you'll look back on and say, "I'm grateful that I invested my time and in myself that way."

Don't waste time sitting on *praying* hands!

When my husband first noticed me, what stood out to him were areas I had invested in during my singleness. He read my faith-centered blog, noticed I was serving in my church, and was especially excited about some of my sports skills and love for exploring nature. The time I invested in singleness played a role in my dating. Your time and availability change with each season. Even the Bible shares how our duties change in marriage (Deut. 24:5). When you're married, especially in the beginning, you're spending more time learning about your spouse than socializing with friends. Once you have children, you're spending more time raising little ones than meeting up for girls' day. None are bad but rather

> WE CAN REMAIN CONTENT AND MOVE IN EXPECTATION BY BEING ACTIVE IN THE PURPOSE OF WHERE WE ARE.

unique to the time and focus. Investing in my love of writing, volunteering my free time, and socializing and exploring was to benefit me, but it also stood out to my coming husband.

We can remain content and move in expectation by being active in the purpose of where we are.

EXPECT TO KEEP GOING

I'll admit I become very passionate about getting back in shape and creating a gym routine after a season of losing strength or after a pregnancy. Motivation comes, and I hit the ground running! Eager to see results, I start back on fire and ready to get consistent with my routine. However, when results came slowly—or when I reached my goals too quickly—my passion would fade. But for sustainable health and strength, fitness must remain a lifestyle rather than a spike of interest. The same is true for prayer.

"Do not despise these small beginnings, for the LORD rejoices to see the work begin." (Zech. 4:10 NLT)

Our prayers should not slow down, lose passion, or dispel hope, like my enthusiasm for and commitment to the gym did. Whenever I'd lose motivation, I'd do one of two things: show up anyway and be more encouraged as I worked out, or refuel the vision and find my motivation again. On days that you're feeling reluctant or lost in prayer, I want you to keep showing up and find your passion as you pray fervently without ceasing, or regrip your focus by revisiting the vision.

Upon repeating the same prayers, doubt would tell us our prayers are not "working," but I beg to differ. I believe they're simply building. We are encouraged to not grow tired in praying, to continuously come before God with our petitions (1 Thess. 5:16–18). Just like each trip to the gym builds a little more muscle and burns a few more calories, each prayer reconnects us with the God who is above it all. Nothing is over or hopeless when He is in it!

One day when you look back on past seasons, you will see your large, numerous, and constant prayers as a sweet remembrance in the building of the things you have been praying toward. I reread the prayers and sentiments I wrote down in my season of singleness now with such fondness.

Take a moment now and thank God for every prayer of yours He has listened to and taken to heart, and for all the ways He's answered them—seen and unseen, known and not yet known.

There are two things I want you to keep in mind as you continue to pray with expectation:

1. **You can say what you see, or you can pray what you seek.** This applies to any area of life. Are you stuck in singleness or are you on an adventure through waiting? Are there no good guys left or is there a perfect guy tucked away for you? Is the current trial you're walking through wearing you down or are you building new faith muscles? Has God singled you out or are you waiting for the single best path He has for you? This will serve you well in your marriage but also in your friendships, career, and all other areas of life. When we tune our hearts and minds to the Lord, He shapes our words and outlook.
2. **Your perspective is shifted through prayer.** Through prayer our minds are renewed and our speech refined. This transforms how we perceive and respond to things and people around us.

- Circumstances become opportunities
- Failure becomes teaching
- Criticism becomes advice

- Delay becomes small progress
- Waiting becomes preparation

Speak life over your husband today and let prayer be the anchor to shape the direction for your thoughts and words.

DECLARE EVEN DESPITE

On our calendars, every Thursday night has the same reminder: "Date night." It's a highlight of the week for Arden and me as we look forward to connecting after workdays and life's demands. Sometimes we stay in and watch a movie, and other nights we get dressed up and try a new restaurant. In Nashville, where we live, there are tons of restaurants on our "to-try" list. But sometimes I think we're not qualified to try them. Not because we're not trendy enough for the hip city spots (which could still be true) but because some of the menus are too adventurous for us to feel confident ordering.

This esteemed dining comes with dishes inspired from all around the world. But not only are the flavors and ingredients foreign-influenced; so are the names. You may see something that sounds delicious but have no idea how to pronounce it. For me, if I see words like *bouillabaisse*, *foie gras*, or *arancini* as dinner options, I will undoubtedly resort to pointing to them on the menu when ordering rather than butchering the pronunciation and feeling awkward and embarrassed.

Praying for your future husband can be awkward at first, but I want you to pray despite any awkwardness, timidity, or nay-saying.

Even if you're a longtime pray-er, lifting prayers for someone you want to know but do not yet can feel foreign at first, like those foreign dishes. I'll admit I felt uneasy and nervous when I started praying for my husband back when I was single. There was the beginning hesitation that came with uncertainty. I didn't know my future husband's name, current needs, or prayer requests. Whenever I'd prayed for someone before, I'd used those three areas as my prayer road map. I could pray with clear direction such as, "Lord, in Your grace please help Jennifer overcome this sickness. Take away her fever and give her strength. Amen." Easy.

But there's an invitation where it's not so easy; past the awkward and unknown lies new things to find—faith and fun!

It took a while for me to find my rhythm when I first started praying for my future husband. I began by highlighting verses here or there I thought would be beneficial to a man. Then eventually I started praying specific prayers, prophesying over his life, and writing him love letters. This act of love and faith can be daunting at first, sure, but as you step out and get your feet wet, I believe you, too, will unlock your own hidden arena to effectively go to war for your future partner and your marriage.

The more time I spent praying for my unrevealed spouse, the more I braved the uncertainty and welcomed the process. I became more and more accustomed to these future-oriented prayers and settled into a comfort with them. My awkwardness in praying for "so and so" transformed to a sweet challenge of sorts. I began to feel excited that I had the chance to pray for something and someone presently unknown.

For we know in part and we prophesy in part. (1 Cor. 13:9)

It's so tempting to shy away from prayer, whether praying for our future spouses or praying for strangers, because we fear we have to get it perfect. I'm comforted by 1 Corinthians 13:9 that the heart of prayer is to grow in our faith as we develop our prayer muscles. We're not expected to know it all, but rather to run to the One who does! God is all-knowing, and prayer is our communication and participation in His glorious plans.

There were nights my prayers for my now-spouse were simple,

asking God to be with him or to simply bless him. Then there were days that through His direction I'd war for him in ways that surprised me. Later in our engagement, I'd learn of the times of trial Arden had walked through and be in awe of how those Spirit-led prayers aligned with what he was facing.

When it comes to praying for your future husband, the goal is not to ascertain a name or get answers quickly. Remember that you're praying with God. He knows who your future spouse is, when you will meet, and all the details. As our first love, God is our first priority.

A MATTER OF TIME

How often can we pray for our husbands? We don't want to make them an idol, but we also don't want to miss a chance to intercede on his/our behalf. So just how frequently are we allowed to lift our future spouses up to God? I daresay there is no limit.

If prayer is a conversation with God, I don't want to cut that communication off.

Instead of managing the minutes in prayer for our future husbands, I'd compare the percent. If the majority of our time in prayer is us asking God for things for ourselves or things for our husbands, we should alter our time and agenda. The Bible says let us first enter His courts with praise (Ps. 100:4). Meaning, we should come to prayer with a list of ways to praise God, not a list of things to ask Him for. Then our hearts will be in a posture of gratitude and reverence, and what we ask for will be under the mantle of His will and in full belief. This is how we can be content in our season and have hope even while waiting on the answer.

When it comes to prayer, our time should not have to be capped.

I don't believe you can go wrong praying for your future husband daily *if* you're praying through gratitude *and* you are praying about other areas of your life throughout the day.

I aim to pray for my husband, and now our kids as well, daily. Some days that's an hour sitting by the fire with worship music on, other days it may be five minutes while making lunch or running errands. I want our prayer lives to be consistent, not complicated.

What should our aim be when praying for our future husbands? Let's seek to be women who pray thankful, consistent, faith-filled prayers.

When we pray over any area, we are declaring God's powerful promises and inviting His might into our circumstances. Here are three scriptures to declare in expectation over your future marriage:

1. My husband and I will not be torn apart.

   "So they are no longer two but one flesh. What therefore God has joined together, let not man separate" (Matt. 19:6).

2. We will not be forsaken.

   "When you pass through the waters, I will be with you; and when you pass through the rivers, they will not sweep over you" (Isa. 43:2 NIV).

3. We will remain protected and united as we remain in Him.

   "Though one may be overpowered, two can defend themselves. A cord of three strands is not quickly broken" (Eccl. 4:12 NIV).

As you pray and believe for marriage, don't simply ask for a relationship but believe for one rich in power! Speaking God's Word and pronouncing His truths aloud through declaration aligns your relationship with God's promises. Let your partnership be strengthened and your heart secure by meditating on God's Word, making it a lamp to your feet and an anthem over every part of your relationship.

CHAPTER 12

PRAY WITH DISCERNMENT

I can recall playing "red light, green light" as a kid at recess. The game's objective: Don't get caught moving forward when you're not permitted to. The person calling the shots would yell out one of two things: "green light," permitting participants to move forward, or "red light," making them quickly halt. Whenever the leaders were turned around and the light was green, you had to run as fast as you could while unseen, but the trick was knowing how fast was too fast so that you could stop when needed. You had to thoughtfully judge, based on the person's patterns and pace, how much you could move ahead without going so fast that you'd get caught moving at the wrong time.

Thankfully, our God is fatherly and doesn't deal with us like we're playing grade school games. He's not looking to trap us or catch us off guard. But He can and does actively give us direction and advisement on when we should be on the move and when we should pause. Almost like heavenly green lights and red lights, telling us when to go or not.

Switching from lights to flags, let's talk about red flags and green flags when it comes to potential partners. Green flags could be that a man is kind to his mother, active in the church, and quick to listen, while red flags could be he's not confident that he's ready for a serious relationship, he doesn't take ownership of mistakes or situations, and he wears socks with sandals (kidding, but not kidding). These flags are obvious and distinguishable. These are great for making informed decisions and choosing direction in the beginning of a relationship. Yet they leave us wondering about the middle ground.

What do you do once you've checked there are no obvious red flags about this guy and ensured he waves green flags instead? The truth is that even seemingly good people, ones without glaring red flags, don't necessarily deserve our "yes." Sometimes what feels like a good option can be simply that—good. But that doesn't mean it's God's best. Before you start a relationship, do you have a green light?

When I was in college, I stepped away from a relationship I knew was not glorifying God. It wasn't easy to let go of, but I could no longer overlook the red flags that had become glaring. While this person was kind and talented, he was not a believer or in alignment with the vision I had for marriage. Like many of us have at some point, I found myself focusing on the good and forgoing looking for his godly fruit. Friend, that always comes at a cost for both people involved. So I had to make a choice: Was I going to let go of my hope for the marriage I'd envisioned or let go of this relationship?

Thanks to a handful of amazing, no-nonsense girlfriends, I chose the latter and was able to close that door. These women were instrumental in my choices and steps after that tough breakup—lovingly prying my phone out of my hands when I considered texting him again and instead pointing me back to Jesus (and a few comfort snacks).

Eventually, after some much-needed heart work and lots of late-night girl chats and prayers, the thought of dating again slowly started to seem plausible. When a guy from church asked me on a date, my friends were all for it. Honestly, I think they were so hopeful I would keep my eyes set on a good Christian guy instead of running back to "my type" that they were more on board than I was. And I get where they were coming from, but I wasn't exactly . . . excited.

Now, this guy was friendly, cute, and did love Jesus, but there was something *missing*. In my heart and spirit, I knew that while he was a pleasant person to be around, he didn't feel like *my* person to date.

"Just give it a try; he's a good guy." "This could be good for you," my friends said.

But I didn't want *good for me*. I wanted *great for me*—to feel strongly about my next relationship, beginning to end. I love that they were trying to guard my heart and steer me in the right direction; however, there are not a limited number of good men left, and we should not have to force a relationship with a fellow believer to have a godly marriage. Just because someone is a good catch doesn't mean they're your future spouse—and that's okay. We don't have to panic-pick the first cute Christian we see like it's a biblical version of musical chairs.

There must be an account for personalization in unions. God is the best matchmaker because He formed us—He knows us inside and out. I believe that there are good options and there are godly options. The latter may be the ones that surprise us or cause us to spend a little more time waiting, but God's best is always the better choice.

To know whether to move forward in a relationship, you need discernment.

And this is my prayer: that your love may abound more and more in knowledge and depth of insight, so that you may be able to discern what is best. (Phil. 1:9–10 NIV*)*

Think of driving, for example. You have to be able to discern a green light from a yellow and red light. To keep traffic flowing and ensure safety (for yourself and others), you have to know when to drive forward, when to pause, and when to stop. Likewise, prayer is a vehicle for discernment in dating. It will help you be focused in where you're going and discern what signals God is showing you when it comes to a potential partner!

At the end of the day, you have to decide what you discern. My friends had good intentions in that circumstance, but I didn't feel the green light for a date. Other times I drove right through a red light even when friends saw and tried to warn me. Discernment is like your spiritual GPS—it doesn't just keep you on the right road; it also helps you avoid collisions. If you're ever unsure whether it's a red or green moment, treat it like a yellow: Slow down, pray up, and proceed with caution. Because the last thing you want to do is speed ahead or slam on the brakes and end up in a fender bender of the heart.

So stay tuned to what God's showing you. Sometimes He'll say "go," and other times "stop"—but His timing is always perfect. And when the light finally turns green? You'll know. It'll be worth the wait, worth the lessons, and yes, even worth the detours. So throw on your favorite playlist, roll the windows down, and enjoy the ride.

HOW TO DISCERN

After living in a few different areas of Nashville, we finally found a place to call home in 2022. It took a few months of exploring, but I began feeling familiar with the lay of the land and relied less and less on my GPS to find gas stations or get me to the grocery store.

Call it getting old, a habit—whatever—but even after I knew how to get places, I'd still find myself plugging in the directions when I got behind the wheel. I usually knew the way to where I was going, but I was still comforted by having the directions *jussssst* in case there was a wreck along the way or I wasn't paying attention because I was jamming too passionately to my favorite song (you know how the car can turn into a concert real fast).

Even if I'm following a familiar direction in life or making a decision that seems like a no-brainer, I still want to ask for God's direction and discernment.

Because I'm me, and He is Him. I can still get it wrong, even after years of getting it right. His understanding far surpasses my own, and if we have the ability to ask Him for direction, why would we ever stop?

Especially in the realm of relationships, the path to finding your spouse can seem sure and steady one day, then bring you to a closed route the next. But being led by heavenly discernment through prayer will keep you headed in the right direction.

So what is discernment, and how do we get it?

Essentially, discernment is the ability to perceive and make good decisions. If we break it down further, we find two origins for the word in Hebrew and Greek:

- *bin* or *biyn* (Hebrew)—to understand, perceive, consider[1]
- *diakrisis* (Greek)—disputation, to judge or distinguish between things[2]

Discernment is a combination of understanding the knowledge we have been given and using wisdom to perceive what to do and judge what is best. A discerning woman has matured in her own knowledge, held God's Word in her heart, and is listening for His instruction. Though she may be able, she doesn't make decisions alone. See, the Lord grants us free will in our choices, but if we are wise, we lean on His leading to make our decisions.

"I will instruct you and teach you in the way you should go;
I will counsel you with my eye upon you." (*Ps. 32:8*)

Once my husband and I were married, my in-laws told us they would not intervene in our marriage, but they were always there if we needed advice. They knew their little boy had become a husband, and as a new couple we were learning things for ourselves. As they explained it, their position was no longer his supervisors but now our advocates. Should we ever need advice, wisdom, or help—they were ready to give it; all we needed to do was ask.

We may be wise in our own nature and mature from years of walking faithfully, but we never outgrow our need for God's counsel, nor does the benefit we receive from it lessen. We discern by being near and knowledgeable.

In God's goodness, He illuminates the best paths for us *if* we ask for His advice. He is a counselor but also a responder—He waits to be invited. We supplicate for direction and the Lord supplies discernment.

Discernment is an understanding that surpasses our own knowledge. We don't *have* discernment; we *receive* discernment. True wisdom is found on a bridge of trust in and knowledge of God's Word. That's where the Holy Spirit speaks and offers whispers of direction.

To summarize, discernment is:

- **Spirit-led**: It's given by the Holy Spirit and not reliant on our own wisdom.
- **Truth-based**: It's rooted in the Word over feelings, opinions, or comforts.
- **Purposeful**: It helps believers live in a way that honors and glorifies God.

WE DON'T *HAVE* DISCERNMENT; WE *RECEIVE* DISCERNMENT.

Now that we understand discernment is from the Lord and brought from asking for it in prayer, let's talk about what it looks like when supplied.

WHAT DOES DISCERNMENT LOOK LIKE?

Discernment of where God is and is not leading you is revealed in many ways. A strong discernment can come from a spoken word or notable sign, or it can come from the peace that does or doesn't arise in a decision. Direction can be derived from what we've studied in Scripture or what we sense in prayer. John 16 tells us that the Holy Spirit is our guide. When we don't know the way to go, the Spirit leads us in truth. He reveals answers, options, and possibilities to us, but those aren't always super clear.

Jeremiah 33:3 says, "Call to me and I will answer you, and will tell you great and hidden things that you have not known." *Hidden things* implies that we must lean in to hear these whispers and signals. The Lord's discernment may not always come through a burning bush or fire from heaven. (Thanks for making it look easy, Moses and Elijah!)

A whisper or secret denotes a trusted relationship. Who do you tell your secrets to? You share details on what you like to your friends, but only what you love to your best friends. You'll discuss a little bit about yourself on a first date, but only the deeper parts of your heart with your fiancé. Closeness allows for more confidential information. When we are close to God, we step into a deeper trust and understanding, allowing us to better articulate His voice and understand His ways. As we ask for discernment, we should also search it out. Let's not shrink back because of God's mystery but rather draw near because of it!

If you want to know whether something you're sensing is simply a good idea or true discernment, use these five practical steps:

1. **Test it in Scripture.** How does this align with the Word? Test and see if there's any contradiction. *All* of Scripture is living and instructive, not refuting itself but coming together to rightly lead us (2 Tim. 3:16).
2. **Check your peace.** This step has become unduly used today,

but that's when it is the *first* or *only* step in our determination process. Peace should be a confirmation, not a clarification. If something inside feels unsteady, stop or pause (1 Kings 3:9).

3. **Ask wise counsel.** You know the Word and Jesus and so do those you trust. Together, judge and sense if this is the will of the Lord (Prov. 15:22).
4. **Take it deeper.** What would following this path entail? Would it lead to a sticky situation or potentially problematic patterns? Discernment sets us on a path toward goodness and increase, not demise. If you see red flags ahead, slow down (1 Thess. 5:20–22).
5. **Assess yourself.** As we mentioned, hidden insight comes through relationship. How have you been spending your time and processing? Have you been in your own head or talking mostly to friends, or have you brought this situation to the Lord and spent time speaking with Him (Ps. 145:18)?

Through praying for your future relationship, you are inviting God to lead you—and your person—even before you meet. In the midst of living out your singleness with purpose, navigating dating with wisdom, or preparing your heart for marriage, prayer is where we lay the groundwork. Asking for His holy instruction now sets you on a path paved with His hidden insight—reliable and remarkable. Maybe you're even praying for discernment right now through a clear sign that a guy you're seeing is the one . . . or isn't. And while God doesn't always work through emojis and red flags, He *does* supply discernment. Sometimes in big moments. Sometimes in little gut checks. But always with your good in mind.

> ASKING FOR HIS HOLY INSTRUCTION NOW SETS YOU ON A PATH PAVED WITH HIS HIDDEN INSIGHT—RELIABLE AND REMARKABLE.

So pray boldly, walk wisely,

and don't be afraid to laugh a little along the way. Whether you're in a green-light season, at a red-light stop, or cautiously cruising through yellow singing, "Jesus, take the wheel," trust that God knows *exactly* where you're going—and how to get you there.

CHAPTER 13

PRAY FOR SIGNS

Like many of us, I nickel-and-dimed my way through college—I made it through thanks to the combination of hard-won scholarships, wisdom from my parents, and the never-boring, always-humbling financial support of waitressing.

Through four years of serving tables, I learned that waitressing was no small feat. It's physically demanding—you're on your feet for hours, smiling while trying not to spill a tray of sweet teas, and rotating orders in your short-term memory just as quickly as the dishes are being served. At the end of a long shift, my brain and body would be saying, *Check, please!*

But nothing prepared me for waitressing during football game days in a college town.

That's when the restaurant would be filled with the rowdiest groups. You'd show up at sunrise with one (or two) coffees in hand and leave well past sunset covered in wing sauce. Let me tell ya, it's hard enough to hear a customer's order over the banter and smack talk of football fanatics, but whenever those customers had celebrated the festivities with a little too much of their favorite adult refreshments, taking their orders became more confusing. I can recall questioning whether I'd heard an order right because it didn't make sense. *Okay, that guy just ordered mozzarella sticks . . . but we don't serve those*, or *That guy is signaling for me to bring him another drink . . . but I'm not his waitress.* Amid all the chaos and cheer, sometimes the "signs" I'd get from people eager to get their food were not clear, coherent, or possible. As a waitress, I had to listen carefully to what customers were saying and doing but also understand what was realistic and doable.

Now, what do mozzarella sticks and alcoholic drinks have to do with you finding your perfect match? Be at ease, I'm not suggesting those are the signs to look for next time you're out to eat to pinpoint your future hubby (I highly doubt that combo would make for good first-date breath either). In the same way I needed to know the fine-dining restaurant I worked at didn't serve mozzarella sticks—or which tables were mine to serve—I want you to know how to discern which signs from God are yours to follow.

Just like in all that game-day chaos, sometimes what we think we're hearing or seeing in dating—those little signs or signals we're praying for—doesn't always add up. As Christians, it's so important to slow down and really ask ourselves: *Am I following God's peace or my own feelings? Are these signals pointing me in the right direction, or am I just guessing and hoping for the best?* Here's the good news: Learning to abide in Christ and hear the Holy Spirit's directions clearly—with wisdom and prayer—will save you a lot of confusion and bring you trustworthy clarity.

GIVE ME A SIGN

When I first started asking God to lead me in dating, I asked Him to speak to me specifically about my husband. I was done with catching feelings, then asking Him to "bless it." I needed Him to initiate it! It wasn't long after when I had a dream that marked His answer for me:

Walking onto a patio surrounded by nature scenery, a group of people started to clap. *What are they cheering for?* I thought. I looked down to see I was holding hands with a man. Glancing his way, I saw that he was dressed for an occasion and glasses rested on the brim of his nose. Then he said to me, "For our engagement!"

I didn't know much about his appearance other than that, nor his name or where this location was. But what I did know was that this man, who I assumed to be a representation of my future husband, was someone I did not yet know and was somewhere I had not yet been.

I believe that was direction from the Lord. A partial answer to my prayers. This man was not any of the guys I had been on the fence about dating, and I realized how little peace I had to continue pursuing any of those relationships as a possibility.

When we hear of someone who heard God clearly speak that their spouse was the one, I understand it can be challenging. It gives rise to internal questions such as, *Do others hear God but I don't?* or *Does it have to be a clear yes or no?* I've found, at least in my own experience, that when I try to force a sudden yes or no, it's harder to sense direction from God. Not to say He cannot speak clearly or suddenly, but it puts me in an anxious test mode. However, when I am constantly talking to God and taking note throughout our conversations, that's when I begin to feel I can cultivate His promptings through consistent whispers. For example, when I was single I did not hear a particular name or date from Him to know my spouse was right in front of me. But my husband and I both saw alignment in things the Lord was showing us, down to very specific coincidences.

During my time going through my Husband Bible, I aimed to more deeply understand the leaders in the book of Acts, how they cultivated and spread the gospel. These heroes of the faith embodied believers on a mission, and not only did I want my husband to share those attributes,

I wanted to carry them myself. Through studying their stories, I gained an affinity for the church of Antioch, which was the first major church of Christianity, modeling the structure for teaching and doing life in community.[1] This was where Paul and Barnabas began their teaching journeys. In my appreciation for the heart and history of Antioch, I made a photo of the site's preserved ruins my phone background to serve as a reminder of the way I wanted to live.

On our first date, Arden and I took time while sipping coffee to share dreams and visions for our futures. When he was sharing, he noticed my phone light up and started studying my screen. *Is this guy already trying to pry on my texts or something?* I wondered. He asked about the photo of the ruins, and I detailed to him how I'd been drawn to Antioch. In fascination he shared certain dreams he had for ministry and how he'd prayed he and his future wife could build some type of modern-day Antioch. Did we get engaged right then and there and start building a replica of the historic site? No, but this was a little whisper of the alignment I felt with this person and solidified personally that God was sharpening vision within me for His future calling.

It's not so much about the sign we receive as it is about Whose voice we perceive.

Your sign could be that your future spouse will be wearing a green shirt and his name starts with *J*, or it could be something less practical and predictable. You may not even identify it to be a sign until it happens and you look back with new awareness of how God connected the dots.

IT'S NOT SO MUCH ABOUT THE SIGN WE RECEIVE AS IT IS ABOUT WHOSE VOICE WE PERCEIVE.

So how do you know if the prompting you're feeling is a nudge from the Lord or your own heart playing tricks on you? Great question. I want to caution you that any word, feeling, prophecy, dream, or sign you take to heart for your coming marriage should be plausible according to God's Word rather than your own wishes, feelings, or fears.

When we find ourselves leaning into a sign that seems counter to God's biblical direction, let's ensure it's not our own whims. Because even those of us who love the Lord can be swayed by other loves that contradict His. Samson of biblical fame was no exception.

Samson's story is found in chapters 13–16 in the book of Judges. Samson was a judge and warrior from Nazareth (best known for being Jesus' hometown) blessed with supernatural strength. I mean, this guy was like a one-man army, single-handedly taking down thousands of his enemies in battle, even killing a lion with his bare hands. This was not a man to be trifled with!

Where did he get all that strength? The secret to his power was hidden in his hair (*Mean Girls* reference, anyone?). His uncut hair was part of his Nazarite vow to God to honor and glorify Him. But despite his powerful stature and ability, he had his own Achilles' heel in women. Especially one—Delilah. She was a Philistine, the very people who Samson fought against. They didn't have much common ground or common faith to draw them together; rather their connection was built on lust and mistrust (Judges 16).

When Delilah was bribed to coerce Samson into giving up the secret to his strength so the Philistines could defeat him, she accepted. She began questioning him to discover the secret to his strength, but he lied about its source. You'd think a mighty judge would sense the deception and call it quits right there. But he continued to see her, and she continued to probe. After three attempts met with false answers, Delilah finally found that in her bed his secrets were freely shared. Their tumultuous story ended in the predictable downfall of their relationship but continued with the tearing down of the Philistine temple and city gates.

Definitely not your average bad breakup, but it does follow the predictable narrative of what can transpire when we thwart our commitment to God by being committed to someone we shouldn't. Samson didn't have a glaring sign not to be with Delilah, something like a visitation from an angel or word from a prophet. But should we not account the Word of wisdom as a sign?

Sometimes the signs we need are already obvious.

If you're hesitant to pray for it, that may be a sign you're following feeling over God's leading. A relationship is *not* God-honoring when it's built on lust and distrust. First Corinthians 13 says of love that it is not self-seeking and it always rejoices with the truth (vv. 5–6).

God blesses where *He* calls us, not where we call Him.

If you have found yourself venturing down the wrong road, my friend, all hope is not lost. There is incredible mercy and redemption at the hands of our Savior. But if you are on this journey of dating and at a crossroads, I'd rather you radically ask for signs from God than go it alone. Choose to follow Him where He leads, trusting He will lead you down a path of peace.

On one of my closest friends' wedding days, the group of us bridesmaids gathered around her to pray over her marriage and thank God for all He'd done to bring this couple together. As I got to pray over her, a familiar song lyric sprung to mind: "God blessed the broken road that led me straight to you."[2] We both smiled, feeling the warmth and truth in that simple phrase. How marvelous is it that even when we take the wrong path, whether we first believed it was the intended direction or wound up there from "distracted driving," the Lord in His mercy can redirect us. He straightens our steps so it's as if we never missed a beat.

> WATCH AS HE MAKES A BLESSING OUT OF WHAT COULD HAVE ONCE BEEN CALLED A MESS.

If you're at a place where you've been stuck on the side of the road or going down the wrong path, let's get you heading back in the right direction. Give God your heart and devotion fully. Place your trust in His direction over your own control. Then watch as He makes a blessing out of what could have once been called a mess. Let God bless the broken road, by bringing your all to Him.

TIMING OF SIGNS

So you believe you received a sign to identify your future husband or a descriptor of your future marriage. Wonderful! Now, how do you hold on to that without letting excitement overtake or confuse you?

Let me paint a little imagery example I'll call the "umbrella method" to help direct us. Let's say you're stepping out for the day. You took extra time to do your makeup and curl your hair in your favorite style. As you're leaving the house, your mother encourages you to take an umbrella because she heard it may rain. No view of any dark clouds yet, but mother always knows best, right? So you take the advice and grab an umbrella. Now, what do you do next? Will you pop that umbrella open and carry it canopied over your shoulder everywhere you go? In the car, in the store, even in the bathroom? No, you'll keep it tucked near so at the right time you are ready for the change in weather.

If you had opened the umbrella immediately, regardless of the weather, this would be similar to taking a sign as absolute and immediate—dropping everything and making the sign the only thing that matters at that moment, even if wisdom suggests otherwise. Signs are a way to prepare in your spirit, partnered with wisdom for the right time and place. You don't need to carry an open umbrella until it rains—you'll only wear out your arm and probably poke a stranger or two in the process. Similarly, you don't need to hold open a sign. Keep it tucked near, and when that first cloud, or bit of wisdom, appears, then you will know the time has come.

Remember the dream I had before I met Arden—the one where my future husband would be tall and wear glasses? To me that served as a detail to discern rather than a detail to define. It was *something* to look for, but it wasn't the *only* thing to confirm. What would have happened if I ran up to the very next guy I saw who was over five foot ten and wore glasses, sure he was my partner? "*I found you!* It's me, your wife!" I'd have a heap of embarrassment and likely a restraining order.

Some things are meant to be held gently, not forced. I know a direction from God is exciting, especially if it's leading you toward the man you've been praying for. But don't let the excitement trump the ending. When we let excitement rule us, we risk rushing what God meant to unfold slowly and with care. Signs can be meaningful, precious, and predictive without having to be acted on immediately. If we allow excitement to cause us to skip past wisdom and processing, we may find ourselves forcing these precious gifts and directions before their due time. If it is true and accurate, the Lord will make it known.

Sometimes the wisest thing we can do is hold the sign close, let it shape us, and wait for God's timing. You don't have to worry about missing or mistaking it if you keep it in your heart and keep asking God to guide. At the right time, the Lord will reveal the fullness of the secrets He shares with us. Prayer and wisdom keep us contingent upon His plan and sensitive to the signs He gives.

For the revelation awaits an appointed time;
it speaks of the end
and will not prove false.
Though it lingers, wait for it;
it will certainly come
and will not delay. (Hab. 2:3 NIV)

I met a couple recently with a "God told me you're my wife" story but with a twist. Don't cringe yet, it gets better, I promise! Quickly after meeting, the man felt confident God had confirmed to him this woman would be his wife. The only problem was, she wasn't interested. For years he remained content in the friend zone, never forcing the relationship or playing the "God said" card, nor dating around to make her jealous or try a shot with someone else. Year after year they remained good friends, and all the while he had a tucked-away word.

Then one day, almost suddenly, she realized how much her feelings had changed toward her guy friend. Knowing his initial interest and that he was still single, she shared her change of heart, and they began dating and were soon engaged. It was then in that season he revealed to her what he'd sensed long ago: That she was his future wife.

He had hidden that confirmation in his heart. He knew it was a peace for him in the waiting, something to look forward to, and something that, if he sensed correctly, would come to pass in divine timing. I wonder how their story might have been different if he had taken her friend-zoning as rejection and rebounded with another date.

Signs are meant to keep us on track, not become a fast pass.

HOLD YOUR HORSES

It can be tempting to ask God for a sign because we want to hurry the process, but that's not the purpose of signs. *I've been waiting for years, God. Give me a sign so I can find him sooner!* Having the right directions for where you want to go can save time by making sure you don't get stuck down a dead end, but they don't allow you to skip the necessary routes. Even when you have a map, you're still instructed to follow the speed limit signs for your own safety, and others'. My friend, you needn't rush. Trust the signs, and trust the process!

If something is from God—a sign in dating, a prophetic word, or a call and purpose—we don't have to fight to prove it. I believe when God gives us direction, He intends for us to stay focused and stay moving at His pace, not sprinting. When you sprint toward anything, you may have an initial burst, but soon after you'll tire out and stop altogether. God does not speak to wear us down; He illuminates glimpses and insights to bring us refreshment and rejuvenation.

My advice is to not force or test God for signs; rather, ask with joyful expectation. Ask Him to make you alert to His direction, speak to you in prayer or prophecy, and redirect you if you're ever off track. God is the perfect matchmaker, and I give Him glory for all the sweet little details and signs He gave me in leading me to my husband. Maybe sometimes I got some signs wrong and other directions right. Maybe I even worked ahead too quickly, or other times was nervous to proceed. But God, in His goodness, continued to direct me as I relied on Him. He goes before us and guides us. Now I can see His fingerprints all over our love story and am thankful for every whisper, dream, and moment of peace He supplied to signal us on!

So whether your signs for your future marriage are practical or prophetic, abide by them. Pray for the Lord to direct your steps and the path your heart should take, following your desire to be married.

CHAPTER 14

PRAY WITH OTHERS

Growing up, our first cousins were more like sisters to us, and we acted, played, and fought as if we were. Usually our goodbyes consisted of crying, so sad were we to leave one another. My cousin Madison Prewett Troutt and I were only a few months apart, and our younger sisters, Brietyn and Mallory, were close in age as well. We had the best time together and were almost inseparable.

One day while Madi and I were playing beauty shop, our imaginations were especially vibrant. I've always had long locks, even as a little girl. My mom would brush my hair constantly and gave me blunt bangs across my forehead, matching her own. As Madi started brushing and doing my hair, we decided I needed a new look. So she grabbed the scissors and gave my stylish bangs that rested just above my eyebrows a crooked cut and brought them nearly two inches higher. This look may be in style for some who can pull it off today, but let me assure you, I could not! My hairstyle, which was previously complementary and straight, was now crooked and short . . . oopsie. My mother came in, and her shocked face is ingrained in my memory. I suddenly realized that what we had done in our innocent play had real-life ramifications. Not my shining moment, but Madi was in it with me.

Much later, when Madi and I were old enough to understand what haircuts were flattering and how to actually do makeup, we entered the world of dating. It was still good to be together. Through the first kisses and the first breakups, having my sister and like-sisters close was powerful as we went through our relational oopsies and successes alike. Together, we strived to keep to the vision we garnered of our future loves, through prayer and relationship.

Two are better than one,
because they have a good return for their labor:
If either of them falls down,
one can help the other up. (Eccl. 4:9–10 NIV)

If it is not good for man to go through life alone (Gen. 2:18), then it's likely not good for women to navigate the relationship-evaluation period alone. We need our girlfriends right there for it all: both when you get the "I don't think this is going to work" text and your best friend holds you while your eyes turn red, and when you didn't do your nails because you had no clue there was a proposal coming and she forces you to put on some dollar store press-on nails. Through thick and thin, your community will be a springboard and a soundboard—helping you to rebound when you're brought low and keeping you steady through the highs.

Brietyn and Madison saw lots of ugly cries and prayed with me through the breakups I knew were necessary but needed guiding through. In our lows we would pray and process together, crying it out when it hurt and sharpening each other even if it was painful. We labored together in love, committing to keep helping each other up and reminding one another to hold fast to the vision we'd set for our marriages.

They also stood by me on my wedding day, and I on theirs. We prayed together then, too, in gratitude for all God had done and healed. I've felt the warmth of faith through their prayers in my times of ache with mascara running down my face, and the covering of peace and comfort surrounding me while wearing my wedding veil and dress.

GET YOUR GIRLFRIENDS INVOLVED

Praying for your future husband with community brings a furthered portion of faith and an added ounce of accountability to your petitions and journey.

Friends especially get a front-row seat to our journey. Their opinions, advice, and concerns can greatly influence our dating. When you're praying for your future husband, also pray for your communities.

Singleness is a time for close socialization and allows for more time spent with friends. You will naturally adjust your time to spend more with your boyfriend when dating and much more when engaged and then married. But know the difference in adjusting time and abandoning friends. One, you don't want to leave your girls! They were with you before and will be with you after. Second, you don't want to go into dating alone. Don't be the girl who disappears every time you get a new boyfriend.

Let's be honest, if you've been praying and believing for a godly man and marriage, it's easy to get excited when a prospect arises. If you've chosen a solid community and they're also looking for the same qualities in their partner and partnership, they will help you assess wisely. Like a sounding board, as I mentioned earlier, these people will help you sort through the many voices you're hearing and determine whether a guy is God's best for you.

After much prayer and anticipation, you may hear or tell yourself any of the following statements:

- "God has heard my prayers; this has to be the guy He's sent me!"
- "If you don't get married soon, it will be impossible to find someone and start a family."
- "This guy is too good to be true . . . and he's interested in *me*?"
- "I must be the reason none of the other relationships worked out."
- "No one has asked me out in the past; I doubt he will either. I should just forget it."
- "You're moving into a new season too quickly."

These are not matter-of-fact ideas that allow for formulaic responses. What may be a "no" for one person could be a "yes" for another. Your background, tendencies, environment, maturity level, hopes, and priorities can affect what you're hearing and what is right for you. Finding the correct response or readjustment from your community takes a true evaluation of the person(s), the situation, and a true friend.

A true friend will be up-front with you. She will tell you what you need to hear rather than what you want to hear. She will help you make the best decision for you, rather than what's comfortable for her (Prov. 27:5–6).

How do friends get a genuine evaluation of your potential partner in order to give beneficial advice? By being around him and being informed. That could include things like giving them a sneak peek, going on a double date, talking through a recent date, or, if you do not have a boyfriend, letting them set you up.

You can have input and friends involved by giving sneak peeks. We do this almost effortlessly in the talking stage of a relationship when we dissect mixed messages with our girls: "What does this text mean? Is he really into me?" But then it's typical, when we start dating, to cocoon—become wrapped up in our new romance and hidden from the world. Everything is new and exciting, and we're tempted to be swept away in the romance! The problem with this is, it can create tunnel vision for us—only seeing through a love spell—and cause us to omit others' helpful advice because they have no vantage point.

Get your besties and your boyfriend around each other!

Of course, you need one-on-one time, but not every date has to be solo, and you don't have to see your boyfriend 24/7—save some of that quality time for marriage. Go on group dates or double dates. Bonus: This helps with purity. No one is having heavy make outs on a group date, and if they are, well, it's probably time to lovingly tell them this ain't it.

You may ask, "Why should I open up my private relationship if I have peace about it?" Well, if it's a good thing, why hide it? Let it be tested! I'd rather have a ton of five-star reviews than no feedback. You may feel peace or have a word from God about this relationship; if so, then trusted, sound advice will complement that knowing. No one, believer or not, wants to hear hard warnings once the ship has already sailed. Remember the verse in James that says we should consider trials pure joy (1:2)? Well, if we can be glad about hard times, surely we can be glad that we have friends who love us enough to bring up hard conversations purely for our benefit.

Friends come and friends go, but a true friend sticks by you like family. (Prov. 18:24 MSG*)*

THE THREE I'S

Let's hypothetically say not all your people are on board at the start of your new relationship. What are their concerns? Are they make-or-break items? Opinions or warnings? If a trusted voice shows concern over one of the three I's—integrity, infatuation, and inability—I'd suggest taking note. The three I's are common areas for concern that our community can help us identify.

Integrity

If there is a question over your boyfriend's integrity due to his actions, speech, or conduct, is this a red flag you may have overlooked, or one he's kept hidden? These are like anthills, easy to overlook at first, but eventually, doing so comes back to bite you. Proverbs 31 talks of men searching for a wife of noble character, but women can and should look for the same in their potential husbands, and in their friends' husbands. Because it's natural to fail to spot things when we're lovesick, let your friends keep watch with you. How does this person treat you and others? Can you clearly see his character so you can determine whether you can see yourself with him? Integrity is so important because it reflects the condition of the heart and the trajectory of our conduct. You don't want to miss it if this is amiss in him.

When Moses' hands grew tired in the battle with the Amalekites, his friends held his arms up so they could continue on to victory (Ex. 17:12). When your questioning gets foggy from all the fuzzy emotions, let your friends lift up their thoughts and views to you to ensure they can give him a winning review. Integrity is not easily faked but steadily built. The day you share your vows with your spouse, you give your word to him, committing to love him well and wholeheartedly. To sustain your marriage, you will need to be a couple with integrity—both toward each other and toward others.

Infatuation

Infatuation can lead us off the tracks of steady love, with our tires spinning out from hitting the pedal to the metal. You can't run on sparks alone! But becoming infatuated does not always happen quickly.

Infatuation is more a matter of the heart than of time. The theory is that the longer you're with someone, the more you truly know them and the less you're duped by who you think they are. But infatuation, at any stage and after any amount of time, arises because we have fallen in love either with the idea of someone or with the mask they're parading around in. Here's the promising benefit of friends in our evaluation: They're not swooning over your man, so they will be able to see him clearly. And they know you! They know when you're not being yourself and when you're thinking straight.

Inability

Inability means falling short of the character or maturity needed for a healthy, God-honoring connection. Think of it like a job résumé—someone might have a long list of great qualities, but are those qualities aligned with what's actually required for the role? In dating, the "role" is future husband. Can he communicate well? Take initiative? Lead spiritually? Handle responsibility? Control his emotions and reactions?

Not sure? Ask for a second opinion! Most new hires go through at least two rounds of interviews with different staff to make sure this person is (1) a good candidate and (2) a fit for the role. Some of the best evaluators are already "on your team." Your girlfriends *should* evaluate your boyfriend. Because good friends—the kind who love you and want the best for you—will naturally size him up for the job. They'll watch for potential red flags or areas of serious weakness that could cause pain later on.

Now, no one is perfect—we all have room to grow, and a good relationship includes growing *together*. But here's the key question in evaluation: Is he open to growth, or has he shut that door? That makes a big difference in how the relationship will thrive or suffer long-term. When you've been praying for a man of godly character, your community will want to see not only the potential for those traits but the willingness to pursue and grow in them over time.

Now, you may be thinking, *If some of my friends or family aren't fully on board, could this still be the guy God has for me?* If you're asking me, I'd say yes, he could be. Because everyone has opinions, and some advice is rooted more in personal preference than spiritual conviction. If someone raises a concern, take a moment to weigh: Is it based on that person not knowing your partner fully yet or seeing something that raises flags? When you pray about their advice, do you sense peace or potential problems? How does it compare with the wisdom of others you trust? Not every red flag is a dealbreaker—but it's worth sorting through what's opinion and what might actually be God's gentle guidance. It's a balance and a process.

When Arden and I were dating, I was thrilled all the parents supported our relationship. He was exactly what my parents had wanted for me in so many ways, and Arden's parents saw me as a good fit for him. However, whenever we started talking about getting engaged, the four parents on board turned to three. My dad was such a fan of Arden but had some qualms about our engagement. Since we were dating long-distance and moving forward in our relationship at a steady speed, he voiced some concerns: Maybe I should live in Colorado (where Arden was currently living) first by myself to see whether I liked it, or perhaps getting engaged next year would be better.

After lots of processing and delicate conversations, we were stuck wondering how to move forward. If every parent supported us being together but one had some apprehensions around how, did we pause and change direction or keep going? We wanted to honor every parent and began untangling what pieces of their guidance were parental foresight and what were more perspective-driven. I'd imagine it'd be difficult for any father to give a daughter away, especially since it was his first time, and when doing so meant your daughter would be moving across the country. My dad approved of my heart's desire but disfavored some of the details, but in our wedding pictures you'll see my father giving the most heartfelt and proud grin. He liked Arden then as a potential match for his daughter, but now he loves him like a son.

As you bring your trusted voices of family, friends, and faith role models into your relationship, heed their collective wisdom and seek out the general consensus. If there are big-ticket items that come up repeatedly, that is a sign to take a pause and reevaluate.

When praying for your future husband, pray *with* your friends, *for your* friends, and *for his* friends.

If we believe in the power of prayer and seek to be married, let's not stop by only praying for our spouses. Pray for your friends and their spouses. Pray for your spouse's friends. His community will show you more of who he is and make him more into who he is called to be. What can you learn about him from the people he spends time with?

WHEN PRAYING FOR YOUR FUTURE HUSBAND, PRAY *WITH* YOUR FRIENDS, *FOR YOUR* FRIENDS, AND *FOR HIS* FRIENDS.

There's much in my journey that I have community to thank for. From walking through my Husband's Bible alongside my friend MP, who believed with and for me, to the days I processed frustrations and longings with my mother, who always encouraged me to keep heart. Even the mentors I had in college or advice I received from strangers carried influence and weight in my mindset and decisions. I love that our community can be unexpected. The person you trust most to process or pray with could be your grandma, a pastor, or a barista.

By and large, my community has helped push me to be the woman I want to be—both in the present and in the future. My parents' and grandparents' prayers and rules shaped my commitments. My friends' advice and accountability affected my decisions. My mentors' wisdom and counsel guided my conclusions. I believe I am the woman, wife,

> YOUR PRAYING WILL AFFECT YOUR CHILDREN. IT COULD INSPIRE YOUR SISTERS OR FRIENDS. IT COULD BE A STORY OF CHANGE YOU SHARE WITH A STRANGER.

friend, mother, and believer I am today because I've journeyed with others.

So while you're praying for your future husband, think how it could also be for the benefit of others around you. Your praying will affect your children. It could inspire your sisters or friends. It could be a story of change you share with a stranger.

Praying for your future husband with others will sharpen your trajectory and harness reliability where you are, and praying for your future husband's community will strengthen him and supply him with support where he is.

CHAPTER 15

PRAY EVEN IF

Some Sunday school stories stick with us, and some . . . don't.

Aimlessly scrolling one afternoon (when I probably should have been working on this book instead), I found a video of a girl admitting her confusion over a classic children's Bible tale. I burst out laughing as she said, "Y'all, I thought it was Shadrach, Meshach, and *a billy goat*! Why I didn't know it was... Abednego!"[1] I get it, girl. Bible names can be hard to remember. But I prefer to call these three men by their true Hebrew names anyway: Hananiah, Mishael, and Azariah (not exactly easier to remember but more authentic). We named our eldest Azariah because it means "God helps." And boy, did He!

In the story, these three young Judean men of nobility were captured in the exile to Babylon and placed as advisers to King Nebuchadnezzar. Desiring to show the power of his reign, the king constructed a large, gold statue in his image for all his subjects to worship. On the day this decree was enacted, the three men refused to bow down to a god other than their own, causing them to face punishment by burning in a furnace. These three men were threatened while staring at a blazing fire, yet this was their response: "Your threat means nothing to us. If you throw us in the fire, the God we serve can rescue us from your roaring furnace and anything else you might cook up, O king. But even if he doesn't, it wouldn't make a bit of difference, O king. We still wouldn't serve your gods or worship the gold statue you set up" (Dan. 3:18 MSG).

Even if God didn't show up in that way or in that moment, they knew He was still good.

What faith! Honestly, I desire to have that kind of hope and devotion. I believe these three imagined God would do something flashy, something large in scale to overpower the large shrine of Nebuchadnezzar they refused to worship. I'm sure when they said God would rescue them from the furnace, they hoped they wouldn't even have to go near the flames but would be delivered from the chains before the heat could touch them. Surely this was so after seeing how furious the king became at their remarks. The Bible describes how the king's face turned purple as he ordered the furnace heated seven times hotter, so intense that it killed the guards nearby (vv. 19–22). Ouch!

These men's minds were surely comforted remembering how God had previously defied the laws of physics by dividing the Red Sea into two, making a dry pathway on the seafloor for Moses and his people escaping Pharaoh (Ex. 14), or when He warned the Egyptians through plagues, casting the sun's light away for three days (Ex. 10). They understood that no earthly element like the sun, ocean, or even fire was bigger than the God who had created them. *Surely* He'd remove the heat from the fire or abolish the flames from rising at all, right . . . ?

But that's not what happened. If that was their prayer, then they got it wrong:

Bound hand and foot, all three men were tossed into the fire as the king and his men waited to see them destroyed. God didn't quench the burning flames or disintegrate the furnace; rather, He joined them (Dan. 3:25).

You won't always be able to predict *how* God will show up in your story, but you can trust that He *will.*

> All the important people, the government leaders and king's counselors, gathered around to examine them and discovered that the fire hadn't so much as touched the three men—not a hair singed, not a scorch mark on their clothes, not even the smell of fire on them! Nebuchadnezzar said, "Blessed be the God of Shadrach, Meshach, and Abednego! He sent his angel and rescued his servants who trusted in him!" (Daniel 3:27–28 MSG)

Whether you are navigating a delayed longing, a situation that seems hopeless, or a dire circumstance, you can continue in hope. But hope is not found in believing we have all the answers; that's control, not hope. We find peace in knowing *who* He is more than knowing exactly *what* He will do.

YOU WON'T ALWAYS BE ABLE TO PREDICT *HOW* GOD WILL SHOW UP IN YOUR STORY, BUT YOU CAN TRUST THAT HE *WILL.*

See, hope is a confident expectation more than a concrete explanation. Even if you don't know whether God will show up the way you are anticipating or bring the answer you're hoping for, you can be assured that He always shows up and always answers.

Be sure of this: He is with you.

As He walked with the three men who trusted in Him then, He will walk with you now. You are not alone. Though the ways, whens, and whys of His answers to our prayers may vary, He Himself does not.

Hope does not put us to shame, because God's love has been poured into our hearts through the Holy Spirit who has been given to us. (Rom. 5:5)

To be able to stand up against so great a threat and say, "And even if He doesn't," means Hananiah, Mishael, and Azariah knew something most did not. They knew they could trust God's plans even if they didn't know all it entailed, because they knew His nature. Their words show me their faith was not bent on His actions; it was rooted in understanding God's nature. This gave them peace in the moment and wisdom for how to act. They embodied Proverbs 9:10: "The fear of the Lord is the beginning of wisdom."

If you need wisdom for your desires and next steps, put God's plans before your own, His desires before your desires, and fear Him in reverence over any fear of missing out. Then His wisdom will lead you.

You may be wondering, *Would it be better to not pray for a future husband if there's a chance I won't get married?* It might feel that way at times, but it's always better to pray. Our inability to know exactly what God will or won't do shouldn't keep us from moving in faith.

"Hope deferred makes the heart sick, but a longing fulfilled is a tree of life" (Prov. 13:12 NIV). Anytime we pray, we're hoping for the latter: to see the longings and requests we place at God's feet fulfilled. I know I am! We strive for that "even if" kind of faith, but what happens if the waiting gives way to negligence? I think of those who let their sickness, hunger, or angst steal their later joy:

- Esau, who traded his birthright amid the pangs of hunger (Gen. 25:29–34)
- Lot's wife, whose temporary remorse robbed her coming relief (Gen. 19:26)
- Absalom, whose grief and discontentment clouded his heart and judgment, causing him to rush into battle at his own peril (2 Sam. 17:14)

Each of these characters faced a real sickness or pain, yet going ahead of God and bypassing His plan robbed their coming aid. My hope is these stories remind us that it is common to feel some of those undesired emotions coupled with waiting on our desires, but ultimately, letting those emotions steer us is a haphazard plan. You may be feeling negative emotions now, but they are not yours to hold. Feel them, then release them through prayer. For while they may be occurring in the present, they are not part of your future.

I know that's easier said than done. I do not know what it's like to be in your shoes—the sting in your heart, ache in your spirit, or strain in your prayers—but Christ does.

For we do not have a high priest who is unable to sympathize with our weaknesses, but one who in every respect has been tempted as we are, yet without sin. (Heb. 4:15)

If waiting on the right thing, even if it doesn't come, were easy, then there'd be no need for this chapter, or even this book. It's not easy. But you don't have to tarry alone. The Lord walks with you even now, wherever your path may lead. Even if that path is not down the aisle.

Paul, who some scholars believe was widowed while others suggest was always single, has some famous verses about singleness, including 1 Corinthians 7:38: "So then he who marries his betrothed does well, and he who refrains from marriage will do even better." As a single man sharing the gospel across nations, he did not lack in influence for the gospel or closeness to the Lord. Whatever his reasons or longings had been at one point or another, I believe Paul received his own tree-of-life fulfillment.

To remain single when your heart desires to be joined with another's may feel like you're left for last, but here are some women who are believed to have remained single and did incredible firsts in the Bible:

- **Mary Magdalene**: Follower and financer of Jesus' ministry and one of the first accounts of spiritual deliverance (Luke 8:2–3); the first person to see Christ resurrected (John 20).
- **Miriam**: One of the few prophetesses in the Bible (Ex. 15:20) and Moses' elder sister, she is said to have prophesied his birth and guarded him as a baby floating in the river, courageously acting to reunite him with their mother after Pharaoh's daughter discovered him (Ex. 2).
- **Lydia**: Affluent woman of textile from Turkey who funded Paul's ministry. She is also the first recorded European to convert to Christianity (Acts 16:14).

Whether you're to remain single a little while longer or for a significant length of time, make your time *now* significant.

A BOUNTIFUL DEPOSIT

Maybe your longing fulfilled is not in a husband but rather a fulfillment, contentment, or deliverance of another kind. All I can say with confidence is that on the other side of the pain in the waiting, is life. Life springing forth with its fruits from patience and endurance. Keep heart, my sweet friend.

Does offering prayers from a vulnerable piece of your heart, like the desire to be married, feel like you're setting your heart on a clothesline with the chance it could be left hanging to dry? I encourage us to see our prayers to heaven not as a clothesline. They're not disregarded or decaying, hopeless or on hold. What if instead we could see them as coins in a piggy bank? When you're putting them in one by one, you don't believe much is happening. But one day, when you bust the bank open, you see a collection of significance and have substantial currency for something new. When the Lord busts open that piggy bank you've been depositing prayers in, I believe something new of significance will pour out of it!

Our prayers can feel monotonous, like we're doing the same old, same old and getting nowhere. But our job is to remain while He goes ahead of us. Not discounting the emotions we feel in the waiting but capitalizing on the opportunities around us. The Lord contends on our behalf (Ex. 14:14) and hears every prayer. "And if we know that he hears us—whatever we ask—we know that we have what we asked of him" (1 John 5:15 NIV).

And if not, He is still good.

As we close this section, I want you to meditate on the following thoughts and questions:

- *Which friends and family members remind you of God's love? Write about why you're thankful for them.*
- *Which couples around you model a God-centered marriage? What have you learned from their example?*
- *Identify three ways you've been able to pour love into others while waiting for your future spouse.*
- *How has your faith deepened as you've trusted God with your desires and future?*
- *How has being part of a church community blessed and supported you in this season?*
- *Who are the people God has placed in your life during this season to support and encourage you?*
- *In what specific ways are you going to consistently intercede for your future husband?*

PART 3

WHAT TO *Pray*

Introduction

WHAT SHOULD I PRAY FOR?

Once when I was lacing up my favorite pair of sneakers, I noticed a slight chill on the bottom of my foot. "Hmm, maybe there's something in my sock." Slipping my foot out and looking in the sock, I saw nothing and proceeded to tie the shoes. But there it was again.

Rolling my ankle upward to examine the problem further, I found my answer. A hole had developed in the sole of the shoe and that small chill was my little toe peeking out. Briefly sad at the sight, my spirits rose quickly when I understood what this meant: shoe shopping.

I consider myself a bargain shopper, with an eye for high-price-tag style but the savviness of nabbing a deal. My fellow TJ Maxxinistas and Black Friday queens, unite!

I knew I had seen so many cute sneakers over the past few months, either while browsing online or noticing them on others' feet, but where should I start to look for my new favorite pair? Should I jump back into online searching, hit the store, or ask friends which style they've been liking? Doing a combination of all three felt like I was simply skimming all the possibilities and getting nowhere.

There were almost too many places I could explore and too many options. If only some stylist could have rounded up an appealing, affordable selection for me personally, that would have been much more valuable. I felt frozen when I wanted to feel fashionable.

I don't want you to be frozen by all the ways and areas you can pray over your future husband and marriage. That's why in this section I've created a guide with samples of what to pray to help direct and inspire you as you begin. While there are countless areas we could spend time covering, I want this to be a Spirit-led discovery for you and your future husband.

I believe God will whisper areas for you to intercede for, but in the everyday prayers, we can look to the Word to guide us. What does the Bible say about a godly man? What does he do? What does he need? What challenges will he face? Questions like these can shape our prayers.

Many times when we're praying for someone, we ask a pointed

question: "How can I be praying for you?" But that's not possible when praying for your future husband. That'd be a little hard to ask someone you haven't met yet. Honestly, even when you are praying for your husband once you're married, you won't ask him this pointed question daily. Even if you did, you'd likely only get a simple response such as, "My job, thanks," or "I'm good, baby."

I don't know about you, but I don't only want to pray for my husband in one area or one sentence. I don't want my time covering him to be an open-and-shut case—I want to see God reveal awe and mystery in that time of prayer. As a wife, or future wife, you can intercede and pray for things your husband may not ever even ask for!

My husband, Arden, is the most humble person I know, almost to a fault. He never wants to ask for anything for himself. It's sometimes frustrating because, as his wife, I want all his wants, needs, and desires met. Don't even get me started on trying to pry birthday or Christmas gift ideas out of him. But rather than get frustrated at the uncertainty, I've recently challenged myself to lean into creativity and be more aware of how he does express what he needs. This bleeds into my prayers for him.

While it'd surely be easier to give God a grocery list of needs in my prayers for my husband, I remember Ephesians 3:20 and lean into the challenge: "God can do anything, you know—far more than you could ever imagine or guess or request in your wildest dreams! He does it not by pushing us around but by working within us, his Spirit deeply and gently within us" (MSG).

We are able to see that aforementioned power at work when we pray for our spouse. Not sure what to ask for? Great. That means you're stretching your faith muscles and relying on God to direct you in your prayers, making space for Him to speak to you. So while there may be days you're not sure what to pray, or others you could pray for hours, celebrate that you're tapping into trusting God with what only He can do and actively participating with Him.

When you pray, you are partnering with the Creator of the universe—the One who created marriage and fashioned this man you're praying for. Here is my model when praying for my husband:

- Infuse Scripture.
- Start and end with gratitude.
- Speak life.

Let's get your feet wet! I've created some specific topics and sample prayers as a friendly guide in what you can pray over your spouse. We will explore eight areas where you can bring him and your marriage before God in the following chapters.

CHAPTER 16

FOR YOUR READINESS

"Ready or not, here I come!"

How slowly the hide-and-seek countdown seemed to tick as you'd race to your favorite hiding spot at the park. You had what felt like forever to get into place—time to afford a few seconds to explore some other areas or suss out who else was hiding where. But once the seeker shouted out those six words, things got real, real quick. Rushing into your hiding place, you may have started questioning your decision. *Did I pick the best spot? Am I hidden or can they see me?* Once you knew the seeker was on the hunt, self-reflection kicked in fast.

The counting down to meet your spouse may feel the same way. Initially, you feel you have all the time in the world to wait. But if you're praying and believing that God will send you a spouse, then the seeking has already begun. Before you hear that "here I come," or more accurately, "here I am," I have to ask: Are you *ready* to be found? Have you done the heart work and the faith building for the marriage you desire? In this last section of the book, I want to make sure when it's time for "ready or not," you're the former.

What determines if you are ready for love? How does one know the difference?

One must *get* ready.

It's not a switch you flip; it's a process, and everyone's process looks different. Ask any group of girlfriends and you'll see they each had different processes and needed different lengths of time to get ready.

While one girlfriend will curl her thick hair for half an hour, another may toss it up in a ponytail and call it a day. And then there's the production of applying makeup, the process of choosing an outfit, and the inevitable rethinking your entire look at least once or twice. Some women may get ready in a flash and others in an hour—but no matter how long it takes, the point is we all go through a process of preparation.

God's plan isn't cookie-cutter—it's custom-made, lovingly detailed, and perfectly timed.

Just like you wouldn't want your date to arrive mid-glam, while you're getting ready, with only one set of lashes on and rollers still in your hair (making you look more like George Washington than Grace Kelly), you don't want to be only partially prepared when God unites you with your spouse.

Preparation requires perspective, patience, and purpose.

Speaking on Christ's Second Coming, Matthew's gospel tells us it will happen suddenly. "But concerning that day and hour no one knows, not even the angels of heaven, nor the Son, but the Father only" (24:36). We cannot suddenly be ready in the moment; we must become ready in the waiting.

It's one thing to know where you want to go, and it's another to go prepared.

In the next chapter of Matthew, Jesus shared a parable of ten virgins awaiting the return of their bridegroom. Lighting their lamps for the midnight hour, half of the women went to wait with a lit lamp, while the other half took their lamps *and* prepared oil to keep their fire ablaze. Those who went in prepared were greeted by the groom, while the ones who didn't plan ahead were not able to meet him.

> IT'S ONE THING TO KNOW WHERE YOU WANT TO GO, AND IT'S ANOTHER TO GO PREPARED.

"But how do I prepare to be a bride while I'm still single?" you ask. Get your oil ready.

The Bible says Christ is coming back for a spotless bride—one ready and worthy (Eph. 5:27). You and I can and must be brides ready for our Maker, and, by effect, we will be readied for our mates.

Blessed is the one . . .
whose delight is in the law of the Lord,
and who meditates on his law day and night.
That person is like a tree planted by streams of water,
which yields its fruit in season,
and whose leaf does not wither—
whatever they do prospers. (Ps. 1:1–3 NIV)

Marriage is love ablaze, beautiful and passionate, yet contained and sustained. Let's take the rest of the chapter to look at three ways you and I can be prepared: have a strong, personal relationship with Christ, cultivate a sense of self-worth and significance, and be unashamed.

HAVE A STRONG, PERSONAL RELATIONSHIP WITH CHRIST

On your wedding day, you'll be surrounded by a company of people who are dear to you and celebrate your union. When the ceremony begins, the crowd will rise and you'll (likely excitedly and nervously) walk down the aisle toward your future husband and a pastor or officiant. Once you reach your beloved and successfully or unsuccessfully hold back happy tears, you'll look to the pastor to commence the vows and declarations. Preparing to join you as man and wife, he will ask, "Who has the rings?"

This is when some couples experience a bit of panic. Did the young nephew acting as ring bearer drop them? Did Aunt Carol forget to place them on the pillow? The rings are among the most needed items to get married! But they're not the most important thing—you need Jesus in your heart before you join yours with another's. He is the most binding part of your marriage.

Changing your last name after marriage is one of the most significant enhancements to your identity and namesake, but not the most. The most significant change in your identity was when you accepted Jesus' invitation to join Him in faith and became inducted into the greatest family tree. Through our relationship with Jesus, our faith in Him, and our dependence on His lordship, we become daughters of the Almighty.

The most transformative thing you can do to prepare for a beautiful, lasting marriage is to walk closely with the Lord.

This readiness is necessary because it is vital for any season—single, dating, or married. Your relationship status may change over time but your status in the kingdom shall not. Far more important than whether you ever say "yes" to a guy is if you say "yes" to Christ! Because when we're face-to-face with Jesus, He will be our sole love and our purpose. Don't get me wrong, our marriages are an exceptional avenue for purpose and growth. But you could remain single forever and still finish well. You cannot, however, finish well without Jesus.

When you give Him His rightful place as Lord over your life, transformation begins. Slowly, your heart and character begin to reflect His. Jesus embodied love in its purest form, being the perfect example of commitment and devotion. His tenderness toward us, as beloved sons and daughters, was shown through His kindness, commitment, humility, compassion, servitude, patience, and sacrifice. The only way we can even remotely copy such a love is by drawing near to the very source. As you accept the love He freely gives, your cup runs over, making it possible to pour back out to others—your peers, neighbors, and, one day, your spouse.

CULTIVATE A SENSE OF SELF-WORTH AND SIGNIFICANCE

Who am I and why am I here on earth? Loaded questions! And ones that most of us wrestle with at some point or another. Here's the thing: As much as we long for partnership, a husband can't answer those questions for us—though the right one can certainly walk beside us as we figure them out. But the deeper work? That starts with us, and it starts now.

We learn who we are and grow into who we are becoming by processing what we do and why we do it. And those answers typically first form in the single season, when we're free to ask: What am I passionate about? What stirs my heart? What gifts has God placed inside me that are waiting to be used? Singleness isn't only waiting; it's planning—a time that allows for discovery.

Through reflection, intentional growth, and prayer, we begin to uncover the layers of who we are—who God created us to be.

Prayer is like a purifying mask. A beauty mask refines the outer self—bringing impurities to the surface and removing them, then cleansing beneath them, allowing for more radiant skin and complexion. Prayer works in a similar way by purifying the inner self—bringing any impurities, burdens, or thoughts to the surface through His conviction, while His mercy and instruction cleanse the heart and soul.

If we confess our sins, he is faithful and just and will forgive us our sins and purify us from all unrighteousness. (1 John 1:9 NIV*)*

After a good spa day or facial, you can see the glowing results, and I wager the same is true when you spend time in prayer. We present more radiant, more vibrant to the world around us. Exodus 34 says after Moses spent time with God on Mount Sinai, he returned with a face so radiant that others drew back (vv. 29–30). You can tell when you encounter someone who has spent time with Jesus and carries the Holy Spirit; they have that warmth, draw, and radiance to their person that is inviting and unmistakable.

You likely can't go to the spa every day for that freshly pampered glow (unless you found an amazing Groupon deal, and please share if so), but you can spend time daily in the Word, creating a divine, noticeable radiance.

BE UNASHAMED

We don't just learn who we are by discovering who we are becoming; we also learn by untangling who we are not. Now I know that untangling can be uncomfortable—sometimes even painful. For many of us, the idea of facing past mistakes, old wounds, or patterns we're not proud of can feel too heavy, too messy, or even too shameful to deal with. Friend, I was there.

Sitting in the passenger seat, arms folded, visibly frustrated and heart a mess, I remember fighting with my then-fiancé over something I claimed to be a problem when really, I was wrestling internally. I kept hearing hurtful suggestions, *You don't deserve a good guy. Shouldn't he choose someone better? What makes you so special to get to have a good marriage?* My own fears, shame, and insecurities I kept buried inside were beginning to drag me down with them.

But here's the truth: Healing doesn't come through hiding. Whether in marriage or in singleness, true transformation starts with vulnerability—with being willing to look inward and face the areas that need grace, growth, and gentleness. As I allowed myself to process those internal struggles, brought them to God, then shared them with my fiancé, those heavy, hidden burdens started to feel a whole lot lighter. I believe Christ invites us to lay our burdens and anxieties at His feet so we don't drag them on our walk. We were never meant to carry the weight of our past into our future.

When you're willing to do this work on your own, you'll be far more equipped to do it in partnership.

The man and his wife were both naked and were not ashamed. (Gen. 2:25)

Marriage is a mirror. It reflects parts of you that you may not have noticed or wanted to face. I still catch myself wanting to hide certain struggles from my husband, but grace reminds me that growth happens when I let him in. He's not just my partner—he's part of the process.

True closeness with someone starts by being honest with yourself—and with God. The more you open your heart to Him, the more you'll be ready to open it to the one He's placed beside you. Because marriage isn't just about love; it's about honesty, growth, and walking through life with someone who sees all of you.

MARRIAGE IS A MIRROR. IT REFLECTS PARTS OF YOU THAT YOU MAY NOT HAVE NOTICED OR WANTED TO FACE.

God has offered us a freedom that brings deep inner peace—and peace has the power to change not only us but our relationships too. So let's lean into it, receive the freedom that's already ours, and walk into love whole, healing, and fully alive.

PRAYER

Lord,

I thank You for beginning a good work within me for marriage. You are the master Teacher and keeper of my heart. Will You instruct me in the areas I need to grow and influence my thoughts and ways? I will heed Your wisdom. Be at the center of my future marriage by being at the center of who I am now. As Your daughter, I seek to be made and remade in Your image. May I delight in Your ways above all else. Though I can do nothing in my own strength, I can do all things in Yours! Search my heart and show me anything offensive, undeveloped, or underutilized. I am an instrument in Your hands. Through Your great counsel, I believe that You can erect something beautiful and purposeful within me. Form me into a respectable, honoring, and promising future wife.

Amen.

CHAPTER 17

FOR A MATURE LOVE

You never forget your first love.

Mine was my middle school crush, Conner. Well, he was second place to Peter Pan in the 2003 live-action film, of course.[1] What millennial little girl wasn't crushing on the blond Lost Boy? But since I didn't know how to fly past the second star to the right and on to Neverland, I turned my attention to homeroom.

Conner had that classic, early-2000s swoopy hair every crush required. I'd doodle hearts around his name in my notebook and blush whenever he'd sit next to me in class. School suddenly wasn't so bad! That's until one fateful day when I was seated next to him and I opened my journal only to land on a page that turned my face as red as my beating heart. Written in bold, preteen handwriting: "I love Conner <3."

Cue internal mortification.

In my panic, I blurted out that it wasn't *my* writing; it was my "friend's," and she was talking about *another* Conner. From another school. In another city. Who totally existed . . .

Pretty sure he saw right through my cover-up, and I avoided eye contact with him for at least a week after that.

Isn't it funny (and haunting) to look back on those early emotions of what we thought was love? Back then, beginning a "relationship" meant you agreed to become boyfriend and girlfriend at recess, then didn't speak again until you "broke up" via a note from a friend a few days later. Ahh, young love!

Those first crushes—innocent, awkward, and adorable—were our first clumsy steps toward understanding love. Just like playing dress-up in our mother's heels that were three sizes too big or pretending to drive the family car when we could barely see over the dashboard, let alone reach the pedals.

Then one day, you realize you *have* grown.

You start praying for a man who will walk beside you in faith and purpose. And as you're asking God to prepare a man for you, you also ask Him to prepare your own heart. Because real love isn't about doodles in your journal or butterflies in your stomach—it's about genuineness, grace, and growing together.

Marriage will require maturity, depth, and selflessness—and while we may not have had the full capacity for those back in grade school, the beauty is, we do now. Becoming the kind of woman who can give and receive love well isn't something we rush; it's something we *rise* into.

Immaturity, even in small doses, can quietly undermine a relationship. What if your future husband returned from a weeklong, stressful work trip—missing you and looking to reconnect—and that same night you scheduled a girls' night out? Of course, you still need time with friends in marriage, but wouldn't it be wiser to choose a different night?

BECOMING THE KIND OF WOMAN WHO CAN GIVE AND RECEIVE LOVE WELL ISN'T SOMETHING WE RUSH; IT'S SOMETHING WE *RISE* INTO.

Or picture this: You have an argument, and he says something the wrong way. He tries to apologize, but instead of hearing him out, you shut down or retaliate with hurtful words to get back at him. It may feel justified in the moment, but what's truly healing is choosing communication—explaining how it hurt and allowing room for real repair. Small mishandlings of immaturity slowly breed misunderstanding—building walls where we really desire to build intimacy. Maturity in relationships matters because your spouse can only know you intimately if you allow space for growth, grace, and honest connection.

For love is supreme and must flow through each of these virtues.
Love becomes the mark of true maturity. (Col. 3:14 TPT*)*

Maturity is the combination of wisdom and understanding. It's an ability to respond to situations with wisdom and assurance from a level of mental and emotional resolution. We need to be mature so we can navigate the complexities of relationships with understanding, reason, and patience. Maturity sustains the marriage relationship we have so eagerly wanted when there are misunderstandings or mishaps. Small acts of maturity build a bigger connection.

Here are three key marks of maturity that not only prepare you for a strong, lasting marriage but can also elevate the relationships you have right now, whether with yourself, your friends, or others close to you.

MATURE LOVE IS QUICK TO FORGIVE

How quick are you to forgive yourself and others? Once we forgive and get bitterness out of the way, we are quicker to see solutions and ways forward. This isn't allowance for boundary lines crossed or excusing without remorse, but if we have maturity and integrity, then forgiveness of the things that aim to steal our joy or connection can be more readily engaged. No one is exempt from flaws—not you nor your spouse. So choose to let forgiveness work to your advantage now and in preparing for the future.

Forgiving your spouse to come—or your friends, family, or peers now—is following the model Christ set for us. Colossians 3:13 says, "If one has a complaint against another, [forgive] each other; as the Lord has forgiven you, so you also must forgive."

Forgiveness sustains two imperfect people aiming to love in the example of perfect love. The Prodigal Son is a perfect example (Luke 15:11–32). After the Prodigal Son disrespected his father, ran off with his money, and turned his back on any kind of loving relationship, he ran into money troubles and was stealing food from pigs. Realizing he had hit rock bottom, he thought he'd beg his father to hire him as a servant. The father had every right to disinherit his son and cast him out when he came running back, but that's not what he did. When the father saw him returning, he abandoned resentment and turned to rejoicing. I believe he forgave his son's immaturity and hurtfulness long before his son's return, which was why he was able to have joy at the sight of him walking up to the house.

Forgiveness may not always be fair, but it fares well with our hearts. It allows the one granting forgiveness to walk in supernatural peace.

I like to think of forgiveness less as a "get out of jail free" card and more of a "Let's try that again." It's a do-over, allowing one or two people to realign and reset. Let's not hold it over them and hold ourselves in bondage; let's allow ourselves to move forward—hopefully learning something through the process.

Now, if someone is repeatedly hurting you without resetting and continuing on the same destructive path, that is not okay. What I'm suggesting is when someone close to us, like our future husband, errs, we believe them when they say they're sorry and believe we can keep moving ahead after hitting a bump in the road.

Jesus implored us to forgive habitually. "Then Peter came to Jesus and asked, 'Lord, how many times shall I forgive my brother or sister who sins against me? Up to seven times?' Jesus answered, 'I tell you, not seven times, but seventy-seven times'" (Matt. 18:21–22 NIV).

I believe if you are reading this book, then you are a woman who, through wisdom, won't chose a spouse keen on gambling and kicking it with farm animals during a hangover. But even a kindhearted, lovable spouse will need your forgiveness from time to time. It could be as simple as forgetting to take out the trash before guests came over or having a moment of impatience, but this act of mature love keeps hearts mended.

If forgiveness is necessary in our relationships, then so is trust.

MATURE LOVE IS HONEST AND TRUSTWORTHY

Something I appreciated about Arden and that set him apart in our dating is he never made me question where we stood. He told me early in our time together that he dated with the intent to marry—with purpose and a goal. Dating wasn't just fun and games to him, or a way to test the waters. To him, love was for marriage, and dating was for finding his spouse. He proved trustworthy in remaining honorable in his actions, clear in his communication, and present in making progressive steps to truly get to know me. I was impressed by his approach, but even more impressed by its authenticity. Seeing his words and actions align showed me he was trustworthy and that if I could trust him at his word, I could trust him with my heart.

Being honest and trustworthy leads to falling in love more easily, but it allows for staying in love too. If rumors come against your relationship, you're separated in times of travel or distance, or you face trials together, trust will be a tightrope to carry you over what would overwise seem too great a downfall. Trust creates safety, security, and closeness between a couple. And the best trust is forged in two people who trust Jesus.

When He is our example of how to walk in honesty, and also who we will have to answer to if we don't, it amplifies our conviction and commitment. In a powerful example of trustworthiness, Jesus told His disciples that He would not forsake them, even prophesying His own return from the grave (Matt. 16:21). Even in the realm of impossibility, He kept His word and shook the natural limits of love. He showed that love is more powerful than death and taught that truth is a means for miracles.

Love does not delight in evil but rejoices with the truth. It always protects, always trusts, always hopes, always perseveres. (1 Cor. 13:6–7 NIV*)*

In a day and age in which we constantly hear of another marriage failing or worry who we should and shouldn't believe, it can seem that trust would be a hard thing to find in a relationship. But I implore you to pray for trust to be a distinctive portion of your marriage! Set it before you in faith to be a priority for you and your husband. As you believe for this, and *trust* that it will be, then trust shall be a delight in your dating and a magnet in your marriage.

In your relationship, you'll seek to trust your spouse's nature and reactions, and also that they are mature and levelheaded.

MATURE LOVE IS LEVELHEADED

Finally, love is levelheaded; it is not angry, impatient, or unthoughtful. In contrast, a love not matured is often selfish, fleeting, and driven by personal desires, as seen in the stories of Samson and Delilah or David and Bathsheba. David's heated romance with Bathsheba was built on lust as he caught a glimpse of her bathing and in his twisted thoughts ordered her to his palace. He was thinking only about gratification in that moment—not that she was already married to one of his elite soldiers or the ramifications of his actions. His irrational, tactless nature of infatuation and lust brought a whirlwind of destruction and loss (2 Sam. 11).

You need milk, not solid food, for everyone who lives on milk is unskilled in the word of righteousness, since he is a child. But solid food is for the mature, for those who have their powers of discernment trained by constant practice to distinguish good from evil. (Heb. 5:12–14)

If our hearts are not mature, we will not be ready for love.

A relationship running on the fumes of anger, jealousy, or pining is quick to burn out. But a relationship is made strong through maturation. Prayerfully contend for ready hearts, matured through wisdom and ripe for relationship.

PRAYER

Lord,

Thank You for mature love. In due time and with wise instruction, You allow us to become full-grown. We need both Your guidance and teaching to sustain the gift of marriage; on our own we are not fit nor ripe for love. But, Lord, You are the perfect Example and Teacher. Thank You that in our weakness You are strong, and in our immaturity, You show us how to grow in maturity. Walk us in Your ways, which enable us to forgive, trust, and grow. Will You heal old wounds and override stubborn habits so that we may become full-grown in You, being image bearers in Your beautiful display of marriage?

Amen.

CHAPTER 18

FOR PURE HEARTS

In my attempt to develop a green thumb, I planted a mini garden in my backyard last year. After successfully tending a few herbs and berries, I decided I was now ready to add to my bunch. Berries are in constant demand in our household, so I added a blueberry bush and looked forward to being able to step right outside and pick them directly from the plant in a few weeks. But I skipped an important step in my gardening prep . . . I did not remind my two-year-old helper of the importance of timelines.

The morning after I planted the bush, I heard the quick thumping footsteps of an excited little boy rounding the kitchen corner, his fists clenched carefully around something as he beamed and shouted, "Mommy, Mommy! I got boo-berries!"

Glancing down at his tiny hands, I saw he had nearly every unripe, green, and bitter bud in his fists. Then our eyes met, and I saw his were full of joy. How could I be upset? He was so thrilled to bring me what he believed was a wonderful treasure.

I knelt down beside him and gently explained that these berries were not quite ready yet. Though they were *becoming* berries sweet enough to eat, they still needed a little more sunshine and time. Though he didn't fully understand the timing, he trusted I did.

A tenderness swept over me as I thought how Jesus must feel when we bring our desires to Him. In the same way my son sought the reward before his wait was over, you may have been thinking, *God, is it finally my time to meet my spouse or get married?* It may be difficult to understand when the answer is "not yet." But just like the child who brings unripe berries in trust and excitement, we can still bring our desires to the Lord—not with fear they'll be shamed or silenced but in trust that they will be held with care and ripened at just the right time. Ecclesiastes 3 reminds us there is an apportioned time for everything. In His supreme wisdom, God knows when each season's time is ripe. In His care and goodness, God has given us ample instruction to guide our way—especially in the area of purity.

I adjure you, O daughters of Jerusalem,
that you not stir up or awaken love
until it pleases. (Song 8:4)

THE THREE P'S

Your desire for marriage must be pure in nature *and* patient in timing.

Every woman reading this book longs for love, but that sweet and tender desire must reach full maturity to become a *lasting* love. If we pluck a growing thing too early, it does not develop into all it is supposed to be. Relationships require patience and purity to bypass fruitfulness-robbers such as infatuation, naivety, and lust. Patience allows us to wait upon the right timing, and purity enables us to contend for our desire to be fulfilled in its most wholesome form.

We do not want to awaken intimate love until it is with the right person and within the right covering. Because we don't want counterfeits; we want the real and readied thing! Lust is an incomplete variation of love. It will tempt us to eat unripe fruits that leave a bitter taste in our mouths, permitting connection before commitment or entrusting our hearts before they've been ensured proper caregiving.

> YOUR DESIRE FOR MARRIAGE MUST BE PURE IN NATURE *AND* PATIENT IN TIMING.

Pure hearts are expressed in a combination of placement, posture, and protection.

Purity Is a Tool of Placement

As a single woman, I do not hope for you to put off your passion, pretending the seeds of longing are not planted, but rather remember it has an awaited rightful place. Your God-given passion is not an on-and-off switch, but it can act like an extension cord. Let the power run to the right destination—your coming marriage. When your heart cries out in longing of the flesh, acknowledge it is a gift that will be opened at the proper hour. How beautiful to have your means fulfilled in one counterpart, and to get to be that for another!

While a lack of boundaries ahead of or within your marriage can put your eyes on forbidden fruits and keep you blinded from attacks, heeding purity keeps you alert and focused—able to enjoy the gifts around you. Rightly placed passion will allow your love to grow deep, flourishing in a fortress instead of growing outside of its safe grounds.

Purity Is a Heart Posture

Purity isn't only an action; it's a heart posture. You may be thinking, *I want to be pure, but it's so difficult*, or *He and/or I already crossed the line, so there's no point in trying to stay pure now*. Purity is not for perfection but rather for godliness.

In the church, purity is sometimes used as a label—either you are pure or you are not. But purity is more than whether you have or haven't done something with someone. Someone could hold a perfect track record but have impure thoughts, or have a flawed past but now carry a refined heart. Purity can't be captured on paper like a résumé but must be lived out. Powerful purity is rooted in conviction, commitment, and communication, not from one sole act in a moment but from *all* the ways one acts. I'm not advocating for a free pass when it comes to purity; I am saying we need to have a higher view!

Let me put on my big-sister hat for a minute and put this portion plainly. Single women, please hear me: The guy you're with must create and hold boundaries himself. Maybe you have communicated standards for yourself and your relationship, but it's not enough for you to set the precedent when it comes to purity.

Your future husband should be a boundary *keeper* and a boundary *initiator*.

> YOUR FUTURE HUSBAND SHOULD BE A BOUNDARY *KEEPER* AND A BOUNDARY *INITIATOR*.

Both of you have to hold convictions or else temptation will keep knocking until it knocks you both down. Yes, it's one thing for him to honor your boundaries, but does he have his own? During the evaluation stage, look for purity expressed through his words and interactions so it will follow later in his actions.

Above all else, guard your heart,
for everything you do flows from it. (Prov. 4:23 NIV)

This is an area we cannot afford to treat casually, as culture does today. The current presentation of intimacy and sexuality suggests people are starved if they restrain or filthy if they partake. But that's not God's nature, nor His design for His sons and daughters. Love is a gift from God. The question isn't whether intimacy is good or bad. Rather, the question should be, "How do we steward the gift of intimacy?" The answer is to protect it.

Purity Is Protection

With the exception of one state (looking at you, New Hampshire), it is the law of the land for adults to wear a seat belt in the car.[1] While by definition this is a rule, more accurately it is a preventive measure meant to protect us in the event of a collision. You could say purity is like a seat belt for your heart.

Purity is protection during singleness and throughout marriage. The Lord's instructions for love are for preserving the gift of intimacy. Purity is a protection method, and God has given us the tools to apply it. Second Timothy 1 emboldens our soul's ability for self-control and a sound mind: "For God gave us a spirit not of fear but of power and love and self-control" (v. 7).

To hold purity near, we must put far from us the things that taint or aim to mimic it. In Song of Solomon 2:15 the couple emphasizes the wisdom of protection: "Catch the foxes for us, the little foxes that spoil the vineyards, for our vineyards are in blossom." This highlights the need to keep a keen eye out for the tiny things that try to sneak in and steal the growing bond and beauty of your relationship—from temptations to rushed passion in the early stages to distractions to look elsewhere in the later years.

A pure heart is beneficial to keeping you from having hot-and-heavy make-out sessions in dating or engagement that heat up too quickly. But more deeply, it's essential to the longevity and strength of your marriage. Purity is a wisdom article—an awareness of how and when intimacy is protected and why and where it can turn rancid. Do not be blinded by lust that masquerades as offshoots of love in dating, for it will steal from your marriage. Do not be blinded by secret strategies of demise that come for your heart, for they will taint your body and marriage. Be focused and alert, ready to understand, protect, and enjoy this precious gift God has given you!

It's advantageous to pray for your future husband's purity and your relationship's purity even before your relationship begins. Lift up your future husband's sexuality and seal a blessing of longevity over his passion. Pray with a vision that with every prayer, you're growing a beautiful, fruitful marriage garden. Your love is growing ripe! As you're prayerfully asking for pure hearts, you are preparing a powerful protection around your relationship.

PRAYER

Lord,

Thank You for my future husband's sexuality; it is a gift from You! While the devil wants to use it to confine him, You have made everything beautiful in its rightful season. I pray that You guide him in a cleansing from anything he has done or faced. I break off the hold it had on him now by the power of Your mighty name. Show him what or who to remove from his life that was a gateway. Thank You for Your redemption, and I ask now that You will show him how to believe for more. In Your kindness, teach him how to renew his mind and bless his sexuality. Give him the self-discipline to honor You with his body. Teach him patience to wait on the best form of physical gratification. Keep his eyes from temptation and strengthen his mind with a vision for our future. Thank You for making purity and passion alike beautiful with Your guiding.

Amen.

CHAPTER 19

FOR EARNEST FAITH

Back in high school, I landed a job at a high-end boutique—which, for my inner child who used to host living room fashion shows for my family, was basically the dream. Surrounded by designer bags and racks of beautiful clothes, I was essentially getting paid to play dress-up. The store was stunning. Mannequins posed in the front windows as if they had somewhere to be—dressed in trendy layers, the perfect bag, and make-your-jaw-drop shoes. Customers would often march in and point to the window display, saying, "I want to dress just like that!" Honestly, same.

Once a woman came in and darted directly for the woven platform heels on display, grabbing the shoebox in her size with enthusiasm. She purchased her shoes, and we thought we had another happy customer. Until the next day when she returned, handing over the box and receipt. I wondered what had happened. Blisters? Buyer's remorse? Did they look cuter on the mannequin? As she pulled the shoebox out of her bag and opened the lid, the problem was evident—the box was empty.

Turns out, the shoes she'd fallen in love with were still in the display window, and she'd walked out with nothing but a cardboard souvenir. In this woman's excitement, no one thought to check that the box had the shoes inside. Thankfully this was an easy remedy and we placed the heels with their rightful owner. But the moment stuck with me. Because how many times do we walk around with an empty box—especially when it comes to faith? We carry the label, look the part, even show it off in the windows of our lives . . . but inside? Sometimes it's filled with nothing but the hope that no one notices.

Real faith takes more than the packaging. It takes presence and intention—the actual *filling.* Because walking around with a hollow version of what we could and were meant to be will only get us so far. As one of the vital components to our relationship with God, faith is an area we should pray for diligently and continually. Because the reality is, you can proclaim to be a person of faith but have very little inside your faith box.

Let that sink in—simply *being* a believer doesn't mean you're *full* of faith. This woman didn't get the shoes by simply coming into the store or checking out at the register, just like simply going to church doesn't fill our faith. Becoming a believer plants a seed, but we have to continue to water and nurture it so that it may bloom. Faith is developed as you walk with God, read His Word, and trust His voice. It's a necessary part of your being and your relationship with God.

Consider Hebrews 11:6: "And without faith it is impossible to please him, for whoever would draw near to God must believe that he exists and that he rewards those who seek him." Let's dissect that verse a little. First and foremost, the reward of faith is His presence—the core desire of our hearts. Second, it says if we are to draw near, then we must believe He exists. Now, it's one thing to believe Jesus *existed*—that He walked the earth and rose again—but the verse is not using past tense. It says that faith is to believe He *exists*!

So let me ask, Do you have faith that He is with you in your walk, in your every decision and moving in your circumstances? Without faith, how can we have confidence to come to God, trust in what we cannot see, or believe what we are praying for will come to pass? Right now, you're expressing a beautiful sentiment, praying to God to bless your future husband and marriage. But how much good would those prayers do if they were asked without belief that God was listening and working upon them? Faith is the soil where hope takes root, and if you want to see God move in your relationships, you must dare to believe that He already is.

> FAITH IS THE SOIL WHERE HOPE TAKES ROOT, AND IF YOU WANT TO SEE GOD MOVE IN YOUR RELATIONSHIPS, YOU MUST DARE TO BELIEVE THAT HE ALREADY IS.

FAITH, TRUST, AND PIXIE DUST

I'm a sucker for classic cinema. I love *It's A Wonderful Life* and *Peter Pan*. In *Peter Pan*, this classic tale of the young boy who never grows up, Peter meets the Darling children—Wendy, John, and Michael—and invites them to his magical world in Neverland. However, they must learn to fly in order to reach the destination. Peter wonders how to teach them and comes up with the famous direction that all they need is a little "faith, trust, and pixie dust."[1] The three children begin attempting to fly, trusting Peter's instruction, saying on repeat, "We can fly," until they eventually begin soaring through the sky together to the second star to the right.

Without faith it becomes impossible to accept or participate in the mighty moves of God. There is no ancient, biblical pixie dust (that I know of) that can increase our faith. But we, too, can put into practice our own faith until we find ourselves soaring at great heights of belief.

Even the disciples sometimes struggled with faith, and they walked alongside Jesus in the flesh! When Jesus was resurrected, He appeared to the disciples and revealed Himself to them. They were in awe, looking over His hands and scars and being amazed and relieved to see their Rabbi again. But one was not present at this time: Thomas.

When Thomas rejoined the disciples, they exclaimed that they had seen the Lord, and He was alive! But Thomas, still grieving and skeptical, replied, "Unless I see the nail marks in his hands and put my finger where the nails were, and put my hand into his side, I will not believe" (John 20:25 NIV).

His response was honest and human but marked by doubt and pain. And yet, when Jesus appeared again to the disciples, it's as if He knew his friend's inner struggle. He walked straight to Thomas, not scolding him, but rather gently inviting him to believe. "Put your finger here . . . Reach out your hand and put it into my side," Jesus said (v. 27 NIV). Then He spoke directly to Thomas's struggle and exclaimed, "Stop doubting and believe."

SMALL BEGINNINGS, BIG FAITH

Faith is foundational to our relationship with God, and yet it's something that needs to grow, be strengthened, and sustained—especially in times of doubt, fear, or hardship. The Bible encourages us to ask God for more faith, just as the disciples did in Luke 17 when they said to the Lord, "Increase our faith!" (v. 5).

Jesus said if we have faith but the size of a mustard seed, we can see miracles happen (Matt. 17:20). This used to throw me off because when I think of mustard, I picture the typical bright yellow bottle the size of my hand. But Jesus wasn't referring to a considerably sized condiment. An actual mustard seed is only about one to two millimeters—barely visible if held between two fingers.

The Lord is gentle enough to begin with the smallest seed of faith, yet firm in reminding us we cannot get far without it. Faith is how we draw near to God and draw protection from spiritual attacks. The reward for drawing near in faith is experiencing God's presence. And it's in His presence we find our own magical world of splendor—a wondrous refreshing of peace, comfort, wisdom, and joy.

Faith asks something *un*natural from us so that we may walk in God's *super*natural strength. It calls us to step beyond what we can see, into the realm of what only God can do. Our human nature longs for evidence before belief, but faith flips that narrative—inviting us to trust what we cannot yet see and to hope for what we do not yet hold. Though our flesh may lean toward doubt and uncertainty, faith lifts our eyes to something higher than our understanding.

Faith is a confidence in what you believe and why you believe it. In many ways it mirrors the faith we carry into marriage. There are no guarantees, no perfect assurances. Yet, based on what we've come to know—through wisdom, prayer, and God's leading—we give our "yes" and choose to move forward in trust. That is the very essence of faith: walking forward not because we see everything clearly but because we trust the One who does.

PRAY FOR HIS FAITH

Pray for your future husband's faith because it will bless you and shelter you.

Times of trial may try to shake or break us, but trust, praise, and awe bring our faith out from behind the walls of fear and doubt. Your husband will need to be full of faith so he can stand strong in the hard seasons. He needs faith to walk in his calling and for boldness to preach the gospel. He needs faith to finish this race well. He needs faith to be a husband of integrity.

Take up the shield of faith, with which you can extinguish all the flaming arrows of the evil one. (Eph. 6:16 NIV*)*

Like a shield, faith protects your husband's heart and mind from lies, fear, and discouragement. By keeping your belief tied to the reminder that God is above all and able to do more than you can imagine, threats lose their power. This is not because our faith makes things happen; rather, it keeps us focused on the One who can make anything happen. Kathryn Kuhlman said it well: "I am not a woman with great faith—I am a woman with a little faith in the great God!"[2]

A husband who walks in faith will be able to be the leader his family needs, the friend others can depend on, and the type of believer who finishes well. Pray for him in this area, full of faith that he is growing.

PRAYER

Lord,

I pray over my future husband's faith. Shepherd him into understanding. May his faith be sincere and rich—ever grasping for heaven on earth. Give him a faith so bold it will be distinguishable even to strangers, to bring souls to You. Let not worry nor vanity steal his heart from hoping fully in You. Shape his faith to be an avenue of discipline and fortitude. May not his mind nor flesh thwart his spirit from seeing the mighty power of faith through miracles, prayer, and prophecy. Thank You, Lord, for revealing the mystery of the gospel to him and allowing Your Word to fall upon good soil in his heart.

Amen.

CHAPTER 20

FOR GODLY CHARACTER

I have a friend who doesn't like chocolate. Seriously, how? I, on the other hand, love chocolate . . . maybe a little bit too much. My sweet tooth has a mind of its own. Left to my own devices, I can easily finish off a tray of fudgy brownies, dark-chocolate chip cookies, or—my guilty favorite—double-stuffed Oreos. (Sorry if I just sparked a craving.) The first bite is pure bliss, but let's be honest: Most desserts are all fluff and no substance. Delicious? Absolutely. Nourishing? Not even close. They're like that guy who looks amazing on Instagram or seems impressive on paper, until you realize he's lacking the depth and integrity that truly matter.

Give me rich character over rich chocolate any day. Character—the mental and moral backbone of a person—isn't just skin-deep or fleeting. It sustains, it nourishes, and it shows up when it counts. In 1 Timothy 3, Paul laid out a blueprint for what true godly character looks like, as he advised those stepping into leadership. But really, it's wisdom for all of us: choosing what's lasting over what looks good in the moment. Godly character includes being:

- Loyal and honorable
- Self-controlled (regularly)
- Pure and blameless
- Understanding and peaceable
- Disciplined and steady
- Generous over greedy
- Reputable and well received
- Spiritually grounded
- Friendly with others—believers and nonbelievers

These qualities communicate someone has God's instruction upon their heart. It should be evident by their actions that Christ's words and instructions have fused with their being and made a distinct impression. Take Luke 6:45 for reference, "For the mouth speaks what the heart is full of" (NIV). A man with godly character has been transformed from the inside out.

TRIED AND TRUE

Character isn't something you can fake. When a man—or woman—truly has it, you can see it in the ways they live, speak, and treat others. There's a quiet consistency to them, a kind of integrity that doesn't need to be performed or polished. That's because it doesn't come from sheer willpower—it's rooted in righteousness made deep over time.

See, a godly man doesn't need to rehearse his lines or polish his persona; his character flows naturally from who he is. And let's be real, we've all met "Prince Charming." You know him—the guy who said he's a believer, but you're left wondering what *exactly* he believes because his lifestyle says something else entirely. Or the one who says all the right things when you're face-to-face but disappears when you need him. That's not tried-and-true character; that's charm and charisma. That simply won't do!

You don't need a smooth-talking, Bible verse–texting Romeo who's afraid to commit the minute things get real. You need someone steady and solid. The kind of man whose actions speak louder than his DMs. Will he be perfect? Of course not. But a man of character will be steady and reliable. He'll show up when it matters. He'll protect your peace, not disturb it. And he'll be the kind of man you can trust—not just with your time, but eventually, with your heart.

A man of character doesn't stumble into righteousness; he chooses it, over and over again. He's intentional about guarding his mind, regularly renewing his thoughts, just as Romans 12:2 encourages. Think of it like a mental detox—he will be quick to cleanse his mind from any ill-thinking. He's weathered storms and stood through trials, allowing adversity to refine him and reveal what's really inside (Rom. 5:3–5). He's made it a priority to walk in holiness, as Ephesians 4:22–24 calls for—confronting his failures, taking responsibility, and choosing growth so he can keep moving forward in righteousness. Perhaps the biggest indicator of good character is knowing it is not found but rather developed. You can trust the man who trusts that all the goodness in him is from the goodness of God!

When the Israelites wanted to be like the surrounding kingdoms, they pleaded for the prophet Samuel to ask God to give them a king. Despite Samuel's warnings, he followed through with the people's request and anointed Saul to be the first king. Saul sure seemed the part too—handsome, youthful, and a head taller than others (1 Sam 9:2). But that didn't end well . . . After Saul's downfall, Samuel was sent to the house of Jesse to anoint the next king—this time one who wouldn't only resemble a king but would have the character of one. As the prophet surveyed Jesse's sons before him, he found seven men who looked the part—strong, capable, regal even. But to all their surprise, none were chosen. Then came David. Just a young shepherd boy. Unassuming and unexpected. But when Samuel saw him, he knew. This was the one. The one who might not look the part at first glance but who was after God's own heart (13:14).

"Do not look on his appearance or on the height of his stature, because I have rejected him. For the LORD sees not as man sees: man looks on the outward appearance, but the LORD looks on the heart." (1 Sam. 16:7)

THE PROOF IS IN THE PUDDING

We need men who do not grow weary in doing good, men who keep developing themselves to be their best—uncomfortable with comfort. Why is this so important for your relationship? Because your future husband won't only be a partner; he'll be a leader, a father, a friend, and a reflection of God's image. And it's his godly character that will shape how he steps into each of those roles. Maybe, like David, his integrity will open doors for him to lead in higher-profile arenas—politics, ministry, or business. Or perhaps, like Jesus and the faithful men in the Gospels, his strength will shine most in humble service—as a tradesman, a devoted father, or serving his community. Through whichever role he's entrusted with, character will equip him to lead with wisdom, to serve with love, and to show up with consistency and grace.

Those who have served well gain an excellent standing and great assurance in their faith in Christ Jesus. (1 Tim. 3:13 NIV)

Influence, skill, and good looks can get him in the door, but character will be what sustains him. Lift up your husband now, blessing him with the strength and character for him to be victorious in what he sets out to do and who he lives to be. Pray these qualities over your future husband so he may be equipped for his calling and stand strong in his faith.

PRAYER

Lord,

Thank You for my future husband's character. Allow him to understand and accept the mantle of a righteous man. I pray his spirit is strengthened in this area, that he would understand the weight of his words and actions. Open his eyes and his heart to adopt a model of Christ's example. Lord, I pray against any type of comfortability in his patterns. Interrupt any area where he has not fully been living out his convictions. Surround him with community that will call these things out and sharpen him. I bless him now and believe You have made him a man of character. I'm thankful for the way he carries himself—that I can trust him. I'm inspired by his integrity and passion. I'm glad he is a man who knows who he is and what he's called to do. Please continue to develop in him a strong character.

Amen.

CHAPTER 21

FOR HUMBLE CONFIDENCE

If you tried to put my husband in a high-fashion, runway-ready ensemble, he'd probably chuckle and readily suggest someone else would wear it better. Not because he couldn't pull it off with his statuesque, handsome features—looks-wise he could rival any male model on the runway—but because his confidence isn't the kind that shines by striking a pose or wearing something trendy off the rack. Yet if you asked him to deliver a sermon to a group or gathering, that's a different story. He would rise to the occasion with passion and purpose. Even if the group was large or he was nervous, his confidence that God would give him the words to share would prevail. That's where his confidence lives—in his calling, not his clothing.

Godly confidence is different than *worldly* confidence.

When we talk about confidence in a man, what comes to your mind? Boldness? Charm? Someone who commands a room? More often than not, that kind of loud presence isn't confidence at all. It's cockiness.

And cockiness tends to be a cover—an overcompensation for something still unsettled or searching. Real confidence is humble; it doesn't need to prove anything because it's based in something secure.

Before destruction a man's heart is haughty,
but humility comes before honor. (Prov. 18:12)

Remember, Jesus walked in quiet confidence. His approach was so countercultural that even the Jews didn't realize He was the Messiah. They thought their king would stride in on a white horse with a crown of jewels upon his head proclaiming, "Here I am, the one you've been waiting for. Honor me!" But He didn't. He rode on a donkey, wore a crown of thorns, and honored those He came to save. What a sobering realization of what true power looks like!

"For even the Son of Man came not to be served but to serve,
and to give his life as a ransom for many." (Mark 10:45)

Christ revealed Himself in intentional encounters. He dined with the sick and sinners versus the wealthy select. He served others on His hands and feet instead of demanding service. Our Savior was confident in who He was and why He had come. Never loud or showy, but through every prophecy fulfilled and miracle performed, He was humble, grounded, and focused on the bigger purpose.

BUILDING BRICK BY BRICK

Confidence isn't believing you have it all or are some big shot. Rather, true godly confidence is rested assurance. It says, "This is who I am, and this is what I have to offer; I'm grateful for it and always working to improve it."

I once asked a group of men what kind of prayerful support they most needed from their future wives. The overwhelming response? Confidence in their God-given identity. These men stated they *wanted* to walk boldly and lead with strength, show up with dignity, and live fully aligned with who God made them to be. But many felt stuck, wrestling with self-doubt and battling impostor syndrome. It begs the question: What's stealing our men's confidence?

For many men, the most common thieves of confidence are external and internal pressures, fear of failing to reach their potential or purpose, insecurities or perceived flaws, comparison to others, lack of affirmation or close relationships, and negative thinking or self-talk.[1] A man with damaged confidence can have a harder time showing up as himself, achieving what he's called to, and even showing interest in a woman he hopes to pursue.

You may think, *Isn't confidence an inside job? How can I make my future husband confident?* As his wife, you will be one of the most influential voices in his life. How you see him, speak to him, and empower him can provide an avenue to assurance or cast a shadow that leads to stagnancy. "Let no corrupting talk come out of your mouths, but only such as is good for building up, as fits the occasion, that it may give grace to those who hear" (Eph. 4:29).

We will build our husbands up or tear them down, depending on how we speak about and to them. As future wives, we can pray for God to remove or override the barriers keeping our spouses from experiencing full confidence. Ask God for words and ways of encouraging him, both now through your prayers and later through your words. Aiding this area can help him significantly with how he feels about himself and how he carries himself. Heavenly confidence in a God-fearing man can champion him to soar in his career, enhance/initiate your relationship, and take necessary risks.

Women don't want a confident man because we need him to be the most magnetic man in the room. We need men who are confident so they don't succumb to anxieties or external pressures taking them away from their authority. Men who are secure enough to express emotion and voice their needs to enrich their relationships. You need a man sure of who he is, so he is sure of his love for you.

We need confident men because they build confident women.

> YOU NEED A MAN SURE OF WHO HE IS, SO HE IS SURE OF HIS LOVE FOR YOU. WE NEED CONFIDENT MEN BECAUSE THEY BUILD CONFIDENT WOMEN.

When you are married to a confident man who tells you you're gifted, loved, and capable, you will take him at his word because you know he believes it about himself too. Sister, I love that you are praying to find a man who loves Jesus, but don't be afraid to pray for him to be more than that too—ask the Lord to bring you a man who is steady, humble, and self-assured to be a confident partner.

PRAYER

Lord,

I pray over my future husband's confidence. That through being found in You, he'd find his true self. I ask that he'd have a confidence created from humility and righteousness. Of all the things he could boast or find assurance in, let them be the very things You've fashioned within him. I pray against unsurety of who he is or what he is capable of. Let him be bold but not boisterous, assured but not assertive. You are a God without rival—show him he does not have to compete to gain confidence. I pray that when he enters a room, he would be so confident in who he is that he won't have to flaunt himself but will seek how to serve others. I ask that his demeanor is of a man reliant on You and assured that lacks nothing. Thank You for the presence he carries and that it enables him to love well.

Amen.

CHAPTER 22

FOR SPIRITUAL STRENGTH

I'm curious, what are some of the sillier questions you've asked on a date when you were nervous? Have you ever blurted out something like:

"Do you think a hot dog is a sandwich?"

"Would you rather have hands for feet, or feet for hands?"

"If you could be any animal, which would you be?"

All of us, whether on a date, interview, or simply a Monday morning conversation before you've had your coffee, have expressed something silly and instantly wanted a "can I try that again?" button. But I'm curious what your answer would be to the last question: What animal would you be? How invigorating to be a lion—or better yet, a lioness. They're one of the fiercest couplings in the safari. And while the lion often draws praise for its strength with his roar and regal presence, the lioness is also fierce in her own right. She may be the feminine one of the two, but make no mistake—her strength is anything but subtle. Her primary role is to protect the pride, hunt and gather, and defend their territory.

We often picture men as the sole protectors of the family—and yes, their leadership and strength are vital. But don't forget the strength women bring to the pack. We are warriors too. We guard the spiritual climate of our homes, stand in the gap and intercede, and we go to battle in prayer. Like a lioness, our protection is fierce, faithful, and deeply rooted in love.

We are like armor to our men—covering them as they face spiritual battles and hidden attacks. Maybe your future husband is walking through a season of warfare right now. Your prayers can be part of his first line of defense. Prayer is your roar, your battle cry, and it carries power.

What a mighty privilege it is to lift up prayers that cancel the Enemy's plans and call on the peace of heaven. When we pray for our husbands, we can boldly ask the Spirit of God to establish dominion over every form of darkness—upsetting the Enemy and exposing his tactics. As Ephesians 6:12 reminds us, "For we do not wrestle against flesh and blood, but against the rulers, against the authorities, against the cosmic powers over this present darkness."

Along with protection in trying times, your future husband also needs resilience—especially in a world that often silently wears men down.

In your future husband's training season, he may face challenges such as:

- Losing a job or missing a goal
- Experiencing the painful loss of a friendship, a breakup, or someone passing
- Falling behind on finances
- Facing embarrassment after something went wrong personally or professionally
- Being blindsided and hurt by another

Times of trials, or training seasons, can develop something stronger within us. Pray for your future husband to not merely make it out of hard times with protection but to learn within them. It's often in these times that we gain dexterity to our faith and fortify our strength.

We are not promised hard days won't come, but we are promised heavenly strength to sustain us (Isa. 41:10). In His goodness, the Lord gives us the tools we need to fight well in the areas we step into or face secret attacks. We do not have to fear because in Christ we are more than conquerors (Rom. 8:37).

Ask for God to give your future husband wisdom and foresight, a spirit of perseverance, and the strength to rise after a fall. Because the truth is, falling is inevitable. It's how we get up that builds strength.

Though he fall, he shall not be cast headlong,
for the L*ORD upholds his hand. (Ps. 37:24)*

GET BACK UP

Job understood how it feels to fall. A righteous man who lost nearly everything overnight, he was overwhelmed with grief as his life was turned upside down by unimaginable heartbreak in his family, livelihood, and hope. He turned to his wife for counsel and support. But her response pierced rather than comforted his heart: "Are you still maintaining your integrity? Curse God and die!" (Job 2:9 NIV). Yikes!

Now to be fair, this woman also suffered, losing her children and resources. I can only imagine the pain they were each holding. But she allowed her despair and grief to give way to greater anger and bitterness at everything, even her husband. And while anger can be a valid part of the healing process—Ecclesiastes 3 reminds us there's a time for every emotion—it's not a place to stay. Healing only happens when we keep moving. If we park at anger or get stuck in sorrow, we stall the process of rising again.

Thankfully, Job didn't halt in his processing or take his wife's pained words as truth. He replied, "'You are talking like a foolish woman. Shall we accept good from God, and not trouble?' In all this, Job did not sin in what he said" (v. 10 NIV). While I think it's poking the bear for a husband to call his already angered wife something callous like "foolish woman," lest he see her *true* feisty self come out, he had a point . . . Job understood that in all things God is supreme and His grandeur and goodness are never out of reach—even when we feel we've hit rock bottom. Job said of the Lord, "I know that you can do all things, and that no purpose of yours can be thwarted" (42:2). As he moved forward through humility and faith, God redeemed him and restored what he had lost twofold. Job's story is a reminder that God never leaves nor forsakes us (Deut. 31:6).

Falling is part of the human experience. But after we fall, we're meant to get back up. In every heartbreak God offers a hand—not just to comfort us but to lead us forward. So when life brings you to your knees, the question isn't just how you'll grieve but how you'll rise.

It's better to find ourselves broken at the feet of Jesus and restored by His hand than enraged in our own will and swinging our fists. Because when we learn to fall in grace, we arise in strength. Your future husband can become resilient through reliance—trusting God in his weakness, and even in his heartbreaks, and counting on Him more than himself.

Whenever your marriage faces hard days or hard times, what will your attitude and resiliency be? When your husband is downcast, will your words and countenance be a sure hand to help him rise again? Your thoughts and beliefs will determine your reactions.

Learning how to rise again will serve your husband in each season. Let prayer be your crutch, testing your feelings and reminding you of the course of arising. A woman who knows how to hit her knees in prayer will aid her husband in getting back on his feet. I believe your faith and resiliency can be a supernatural strength in your marriage!

Prayer produces perseverance. Pray for your husband to have strength in trials that will allow him to meet failure as a learning moment, speak life when afraid, and press on when he feels like tapping out. As you become grounded in spiritual strength, you will fight your battles with wisdom—able to confront the problems or trials that arise together with your husband rather than fighting each other.

We also glory in our sufferings, because we know that suffering produces perseverance; perseverance, character; and character, hope. And hope does not put us to shame, because God's love has been poured out into our hearts through the Holy Spirit. (Rom. 5:3–5 NIV)

Life is not lived on mountaintops alone—where we find life virtuous and ourselves victorious; life is also found in the valleys—where we feel hidden, success is slow in coming, or strength is tested.

Perseverance serves us in all seasons and equips us for many ventures. Your prayers can uplift and encourage your future husband to *keep going*—with faith, endurance, and hope.

PRAYER

Lord,

I pray over my future husband in times of spiritual attack. Whenever the Enemy aims to taunt him, would Your Spirit surround him? Let Your peace and presence establish dominion within his heart. Steady his mind. Fortify the territory You've given him. We proclaim Your name in triumph; nothing is greater than You, oh Lord! As the trumpets brought the walls of Jericho crumbling down, may these prayers thwart the Enemy's schemes.

Amen.

CHAPTER 23

FOR YOUR MISSION

The concept of marriage is wild, if you really think about it. One minute, you're enjoying your own space—a tranquil room filled with throw pillows and eucalyptus-scented candles. Then perhaps you move in with female roommates who share your nighttime routine: multistep skin care; getting into those cozy, silky pajamas and crew socks; and ending the night with ice cream, HGTV, and girl talk. Bliss! Then one day, you're living with a *man*.

Men and women tend to have starkly different ways of getting ready, unique preferences in products, and variations in overall tidiness. You may claim counter space for your moisturizer and toner duo—in an appealing neutral look, of course—only for your new hubby to interrupt the aesthetic with his neon-colored, three-in-one shampoo he's had since high school that smells like "adventure."

Needless to say, there's an adjustment period to your routines after the honeymoon. You may find yourself wondering, *Will he put the toilet seat down? Use my fifty-dollar retinol as hand soap? Or be freaked out waking up to my overnight beauty mask?* It's no wonder that a 1992 book release was titled *Men Are from Mars, Women Are from Venus.*[1] Because sometimes our differences can almost seem otherworldly!

A few years after that book was published, a crew from NASA launched a new mission in 1998 called the Mars Climate Orbiter. They set out to collect information on the climate of Mars. Maybe they wanted to see whether humans really could thrive on the planet. But something crucial set off their mission.

The two teams pioneering the mission were the NASA internal team from Jet Propulsion Laboratory and the spacecraft builder Lockheed Martin.[2] They both wanted to make headway in space exploration and learn about the atmosphere of Mars; however, they were not aligned in their building process. Whenever they created their trajectory calculations for the spacecraft to have a successful takeoff, the NASA team built their projections using metric units while Lockheed Martin used English units. This mismatch in preparations led to a catastrophically unsuccessful launch and the spacecraft's destruction mid-space.[3] Because of their failure to properly ensure the two teams were aligned, they quite literally became lost in translation.

Whether you're talking about partners in a space exploration or partners in a marriage, one thing is for sure: Your venture is more successful when you're aligned in your mission. Without unity, even the most promising journey can drift off course.

A TRUE POWER UNION

We see the power of missional alignment in the biblical marriage of Priscilla and Aquila. This husband-and-wife duo played a critical part in Paul's ministry. He described them as his "co-workers in Christ" (Rom. 16:3 NIV), supporting him financially and serving others in ministry.

Priscilla and Aquila didn't just share a home; they shared a calling. I believe they saw their lives, and marriage, as a mission field. Side by side, they taught, served, risked, and built the church—not just as husband and wife but as partners in purpose. Talk about a mission-minded couple!

Your choice in your spouse and understanding of the influence of your unity can determine your trajectory. It's almost like choosing a car, if you will. Do you want a cute convertible that can't fit much and gets low gas mileage, but is fun for joy rides and Instagram-worthy selfies? Or do you want a reliable SUV that is up for the task of carrying your necessary cargo and able to transport you on your journey? Are you looking for a spouse to make you happy and who looks good shirtless, or someone who has a heart of gold and is ready to change the world with you? (He can look good shirtless, too, but, ya know, priorities.)

To be on mission together, a husband and wife should be aligned in at least three key areas.

First, you must be of shared faith (aka equally yoked). If one of you sets your sails to the Holy Spirit leading and the other does not, you will be rowing against each other instead of together. But when you're aligned in faith, you will sail smoothly together—same direction, same effort. Second, you should be of the same mindset in how you want to live. Ask the hard questions: "How do you spend your money, time, and energy?" You likely will have some different preferences but ultimately should be heading in the same direction. Third, you need to know if you are compatible in commitment. There will be days when you will feel as though you're experiencing failure to launch, when misunderstandings or frustrations want to keep you apart. Are you both committed to working together to see your partnership through?

If the mission of marriage is to embody Christ's love for the church, are you both devoted to doing that well? Are you serving the kingdom better together than you would be apart?

"I am in them and you are in me. May they experience such perfect unity that the world will know that you sent me and that you love them as much as you love me." (John 17:23 NLT*)*

Mission is essentially a fancy word for *purpose*. And boy, is marriage purposeful! Find a partner who shares in your purpose and doesn't take it lightly.

There have been nights when my husband has had to push me in my purpose—he's encouraged me to keep writing when I was growing weary, happily offered to take care of the house or the kids so I could be part of a ministry trip, or pushed me outside my comfort zone when I felt I needed to pray with a stranger. Even when I've wanted to scale back, he's pushed me forward. It'd be so easy for him to simply say "Good job" and leave it at that—but instead, time and time again, he champions me. My husband prays for me, challenges me, and protects me. He steers us, leads us, and betters us. As iron sharpens iron, your marriage can be just that: a sacred space where you and your spouse sharpen, strengthen, and stretch each other as you walk out a God-given mission side by side.

And that very mission can serve you throughout singleness.

WHEN GOD BRINGS YOU THE RIGHT PARTNER, IT WON'T JUST BRING YOU HAPPINESS—IT'LL BRING YOU TRANSFORMATION, SUPPORT, AND PURPOSE.

Maybe you've remained single not because you're scared, picky, or unmotivated but because you see your marriage as more than a comforting companionship—it's also a mission field. I know holding out for that kind of vision can feel lonely at times, but trust this: It's worth the wait! Because when God brings you the right partner, it won't just bring you happiness—it'll bring you transformation, support, and purpose.

Pray for God to continue strengthening you both for the purpose He has called you to together. That could be in the church, in the mission field, in a business, in the home, or some combination of those. Your spouse will be a partner—emotionally, intimately, and vocationally. As you seek to find the partner who will be on mission alongside you, partner with God in prayerfully pioneering a vision for your marriage.

As we close this section, I want you to meditate on the following thoughts and questions:

- *Recall a recent moment when you felt proud of the woman God is shaping you to be. What was the moment, and what qualities of God's handiwork were most apparent to you?*
- *Name one way you've seen yourself grow spiritually, emotionally, or personally in the last year.*
- *How has your prayer life grown recently? Where have you witnessed God's faithfulness?*
- *Write about a lesson God is teaching you during this time. How has it strengthened your faith?*
- *Reflect on how your current season allows you to grow closer to God. What are you most grateful for in your relationship with Him?*
- *What other areas might God be calling you to intercede in for your future husband and marriage? Ask Him and write them down as they come.*
- *What descriptors and attributes has God begun sowing for your marriage's mission?*

PRAYER

Lord,

Thank You for the mission of marriage. How beautiful that we get to be united in a way that glorifies heaven. I ask that You begin giving us both vision and guidance for our purpose and plans as we come together. As You have made us male and female, will You now make us aligned together for Your plans and benefit? Make us strong in faith, with a conviction for how to live and a commitment for the course ahead. May You be our guide and anchor throughout our marriage. Even as we walk alone now, I pray You align our paths in a way that we will come together in strength. Will You speak to us so that we may be led by Your vision for our partnership?

Amen.

KEEP GOING!

I'm so proud of you! You've spent the last 248 pages celebrating this desire for your future spouse and seeking wisdom in how to steward it well. We've discussed why praying for your future husband is beneficial, how you can do it well, and what you can begin praying for.

It's now time for *your* journey to begin!

As you set out into activation, I pray that this book has been an endorsement for you to pray passionately for him, an encouragement to keep believing that God can bring forth His best, and a reminder that you're not alone.

Now that you have been guided in why, how, and what to pray over your future husband, let me share *where* you can. Alongside this book, I've created a journal you can use to capture your prayers and write love letters to your future husband to give to him on your wedding day. In the *Dear Future Husband Prayer Journal* you'll find prayer prompts, pages for journaling, and dozens of scriptures to reference as you bless your husband and marriage.

ACKNOWLEDGMENTS

To Mary-Payne Taylor: Friend, I wish those two young twentysomethings sitting on your bed, pouring their hearts out in love letters to their future husbands, could peek into the future and see all that has blossomed since those first precious prayers. Watching your journey unfold has been a beautiful testament to God's goodness and your faith in Him. Thank you for being the kind of friend who not only has laughed with me through the ups and downs but always spurs me on to live by faith. I'm so grateful for you and love you much!

To my husband: Arden, where do I even begin? Thank you for walking so faithfully with the Lord, for being an incredible man of God and a truly phenomenal husband. Marriage was a long-awaited dream and an answered prayer, but I never imagined just how deeply being by your side would shape me into the woman I am today. Thank you for keeping your word by loving me every day since we said "I do." You challenge me, inspire me, and encourage me—even right now as you're busy bathing our little ones so I can complete this book. I love you, and I'm so grateful to have the greatest champion by my side and best friend in a partner.

To my family: It's not lost on me that you prayed for my future husband before I ever did. To my mother, Sonya; father, Marcus;

grandmother, Mimi; sisters; and the rest of the Jesus-loving, amazing people I get to call family, thank you for covering my life with the Word of God, without which none of this would be possible. Momma, thank you for taking me on that first date with my now-husband and reminding me God can write incredible love stories. And Dad, thank you for letting your little girl walk down the aisle even if it nearly broke your heart to let go of my hand at the end. You've all prayed for me from a young age, stood by me on my wedding day, and celebrated the joy we've had since. I love each one of you dearly!

My HarperCollins team: To the incredible individuals at W and Thomas Nelson within HarperCollins, thank you. You believed in this message, pushed it over the finish line in record time, and prayed over these pages with me. Brooke, Damon, Stephanie, and numerous others—I couldn't ask for a better team! Thank you for championing this message and helping pave the way for it to reach the women who are faithfully praying for their future marriage.

NOTES

Chapter 1

1. *The Princess Diaries*, directed by Garry Marshall (Walt Disney Pictures, 2001).

Chapter 3

1. Exodus 2–3.
2. Genesis 29.
3. 1 Samuel 16–2 Samuel 5.

Chapter 4

1. Taylor Swift, "You're Not Sorry," track 9 on *Fearless*, Big Machine Records, 2008; Bon Jovi, "You Give Love a Bad Name," track 2 on *Slippery When Wet*, Mercury Records, 1986; Drake, "Trust Issues," track 4 on *Care Package*, OVO, 2019.
2. See, for example, James 1:19; Proverbs 19:11.
3. Corrie ten Boom, *Clippings from My Notebook* (Thomas Nelson, 1982).
4. C. S. Lewis, *The Problem of Pain* (HarperOne, 2015), 91.
5. John Bevere, *The Bait of Satan: Living Free from the Deadly Trap of Offense,* 20th Anniversary Edition (Charisma House, 2014), 16.

Chapter 5

1. Skip Burzumato, "A Brief History of Courtship and Dating in America, Part 1," Boundless, Focus on the Family, March 1, 2007, https://www

.boundless.org/relationships/a-brief-history-of-courtship-and -dating-in-america-part-1/.

2. The Sexperts, "The History of Dating in America," SexInfo Online, updated March 23, 2018, https://sexinfoonline.com/the-history-of -dating-in-america/.
3. Emma Atkinson, "New DU Study Highlights Risks of Living Together Before Engagement," University of Denver News, April 26, 2023, https://www.du.edu/news/new-du-study-highlights-risks-living -together-engagement; Allie Volpe, "Why Couples Are Choosing Cohabitation over Marriage," Vox, April 21, 2024, https://www .vox.com/even-better/24127335/living-together-cohabitation-before -marriage-relationship-milestones.
4. Scott Stanley and Galena Rhoades, "Executive Summary: What's the Plan? Cohabitation, Engagement, and Divorce," Institute for Family Studies, April 2023, https://ifstudies.org/reports/whats -the-plan-cohabitation/2023/executive-summary.
5. Ed Bauman, "Studies Show Microwaves Drastically Reduce Nutrients in Food," *GreenMedInfo* (blog), September 7, 2019, https://greenmedinfo .com/blog/studies-show-microwaves-drastically-reduce-nutrients-food?.

Chapter 6

1. "World—Population, Male (% of Total)," Trading Economics, accessed August 2025, https://tradingeconomics.com/world/population-male -percent-of-total-wb-data.html; S. Galan, "Global Population from 2000 to 2023, by Gender," Statista, May 30, 2025, https://www.statista.com /statistics/1328107/global-population-gender/.

Chapter 7

1. Maté Jarai, "How Does Social Media Affect Relationships?," Medical News Today, updated June 13, 2025, https://www.medicalnewstoday .com/articles/social-media-and-relationships.
2. Henry Blackaby et al., *Experiencing God: Knowing and Doing the Will of God*, rev. and expanded ed. (B&H, 2008), 175.
3. Michael Todd, "Rip Up Your List // (Part 1) Relationship Goals

Reloaded," sermon, posted May 3, 2020, by Transformation Church, YouTube, 1 hour, 15 min., 4 sec., https://www.youtube.com/watch?v=88TTZgPrtko.

Chapter 8

1. Generally attributed to John Lyly as found in *Euphues: The Anatomy of Wit*, published 1578.

Chapter 10

1. Oxford Languages, "passion," accessed May 14, 2025, https://www.google.com/search?q=define+passion.
2. "Top 10 Divorce Statistics You Need to Know," Modern Family Law, May 9, 2025, https://www.modernfamilylaw.com/resources/top-10-divorce-statistics-you-need-to-know/.
3. Axel Neree, "Couples That Pray Together, Stay Together," Medium, November 26, 2019, https://medium.com/@axelneree/couples-that-pray-together-stay-together-5afac89cd439#.

Chapter 11

1. Christian Bevere, host, *Dear Future Husband*, podcast, season 4, episode 18, "Does God Keep Some People Single on Purpose? (Mia's Radical Testimony)," May 29, 2025, https://podcasts.apple.com/us/podcast/does-god-keep-some-people-single-on-purpose-mias-radical/id1694220083?i=1000710426393.
2. Bevere, "Does God Keep Some People Single on Purpose?"

Chapter 12

1. *Strong's Exhaustive Concordance*, "bin," Bible Hub, accessed October 8, 2025, https://biblehub.com/hebrew/995.htm.
2. *Strong's Exhaustive Concordance*, "diakrisis," Bible Hub, accessed October 8, 2025, https://biblehub.com/greek/1253.htm.

Chapter 13

1. "The Church in Antioch," BibleHub, accessed July 11, 2025, https://biblehub.com/topical/t/the_church_in_antioch.htm.
2. Rascal Flatts, "Bless the Broken Road," track 2 on *Feels Like Today*, Lyric Street Records, 2004. Originally written by Jeff Hanna, Marcus Hummon, and Bobby Boyd and recorded by the Nitty Gritty Dirt Band in 1994.

Chapter 15

1. Anike (formerly Wande), "Abednigo be like #winbiblestories #christianrap," TikTok, September 6, 2023, https://www.tiktok.com/@anike/video/7275722391228075307.

Chapter 17

1. *Peter Pan*, directed by P. J. Hogan (Universal Pictures, 2003).

Chapter 18

1. David Kidd, comp., "Seat Belts," Insurance Institute for Highway Safety (IIHS), updated July 2025, https://www.iihs.org/research-areas/seat-belts.

Chapter 19

1. *Peter Pan*, directed by Clyde Geronimi, Wilfred Jackson, and Hamilton Luske (Walt Disney Productions, 1953).
2. Samuel Weiss, introduction to *I Believe in Miracles*, by Kathryn Kuhlman (Prentice-Hall, 1962), 10.

Chapter 21

1. Sylvia Smith, "13 Telling Signs of Low Self-Esteem in Men & Ways to Support Them," Marriage.com, updated September 27, 2024, https://www.marriage.com/advice/mental-health/signs-of-low-self-esteem-in-a-man/.

Chapter 23

1. John Gray, *Men Are from Mars, Women Are from Venus: The Classic Guide to Understanding the Opposite Sex* (HarperCollins, 1992).
2. "Lost in Translation: The Mars Climate Orbiter Mishap," *System Failure Case Studies* 3, no. 5 (2009), https://sma.nasa.gov/docs/default-source/safety-messages/safetymessage-2009-08-01-themarsclimateorbitermishap.pdf?sfvrsn=eaa1ef8_4.
3. "Mars Climate Orbiter Team Finds Likely Cause of Loss," NASA Jet Propulsion Laboratory, September 30, 1999, https://www.jpl.nasa.gov/news/mars-climate-orbiter-team-finds-likely-cause-of-loss/.

ABOUT THE AUTHOR

Christian Bevere is a creative communicator, author, and podcast host with a heart to empower others to step into God's promises. Known for her relatable and transparent voice, Christian shares powerful truths through her popular podcast, Dear Future Husband, and YouTube channel where she engages in meaningful conversations about faith, identity, and relationships. She passionately guides individuals in praying intentionally for their future and embracing God's promises. She is the author of *Break Up with What Broke You* and co-author of *I Am*. Christian graduated cum laude from Auburn University with a Bachelor of Arts in journalism. She now resides in Nashville, TN, with her husband, Arden, and their two children. She continues to live by faith and cultivate beauty.

SPECIAL DELIV

Loved what you learned in *Future Husband, Present Prayers*? Want to start a Husband's Bible for yourself? Look no further—this prayer journal is the perfect gift for young women! For those who are single, dating, or newly engaged—wherever you find yourself on the dating and marriage journey—these beautiful journal pages will help you intercede for your future husband now and document the blessings God unveils along the way.

XOXO